The Liverpool Masonic Rebellion and the Wigan Grand Lodge: The Last Masonic Rebellion

David Harrison

Published 2012 by arima publishing

www.arimapublishing.com

ISBN 978 1 84549 561 9

© David Harrison 2012

Printed and bound in the United Kingdom

Typeset in Garamond

arima publishing
ASK House, Northgate Avenue
Bury St Edmunds, Suffolk IP32 6BB
t: (+44) 01284 700321
www.arimapublishing.com

This book is dedicated to rebels everywhere

'*Do not go gentle into that good night.*
Rage, rage against the dying of the light.'

Dylan Thomas

As a non-Mason who is interested in history, social movements, the rise of new religious sects and the occult, I recommend this book without reservation - and indeed anything Harrison writes on the subject.

David M. Kinchen, Book critic for the Huntington News Network
(www.huntingtonnews.net)

In the latest offering from Dr. David Harrison, he returns to his historical Masonic bailiwick of North England, where with customary deep research and shrewd analysis, he uncovers the reasons for, and the characters behind the 19th century Masonic rebellion which took place in that part of the country, and which led to the formation of the Grand Lodge of Wigan. Incensed by what they considered unnecessary intervention in their affairs by elitist Masons in London, charismatic, aggressive, and determined Masons in Liverpool and Wigan determined to break away from the mainstream, to form their own Grand Body and return to their pre-1813 'Antient' customs and usages; which they hoped would spread nationally. Harrison demonstrates vividly how the character traits of the men behind the move, not only helped fire the rebellion, but determined how it ultimately played out. What the book documents is nothing more or less than class warfare, fought within a Masonic landscape of competing traditions.

Kenneth C. Jack, Masonic Historian – *Ashlar, Masonic Magazine,*
Scottish Rite Journal

The Grand Lodge system which has served Freemasonry so well for the past 200 years seems, to many of us, to have been the norm from time immemorial. Information about the period from the first Grand Lodge in 1717 until the unification of the United Grand Lodge of England in 1813 has been well studied and widely disseminated. Dr. Harrison in his new book reveals that the strife of transition to centralized authority did not indeed end in 1813. His detailed account of how resistance to centralized authority continued well after the unification is both fascinating and educational. I recommend this book to anyone interested in the transitions the craft has been through and what these lessons may hold for the future as he who ignores history is often doomed to repeat it.

John L. Palmer, Editor - *Knight Templar Magazine*

Contents

Map of Lancashire 9

Abbreviations 11

Acknowledgements 13

Foreword 15

Introduction 17

Chapter One
The beginning of the rebellion 27

Chapter Two
The rebel Grand Lodge in Liverpool 45

Chapter Three
The Wigan Grand Lodge 53

Chapter Four
The end of the 'Antients' 63

Chapter Five
Life after the rebellion 75

Conclusion 87

Appendix I 89

Appendix II 97

Appendix III 99

Bibliography 101

Index 111

Map of Lancashire

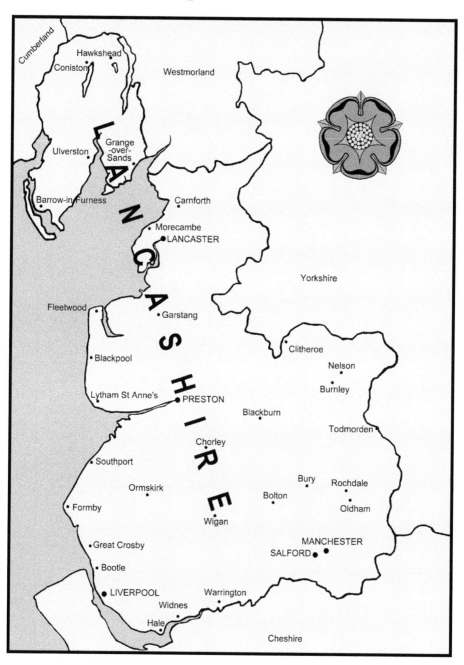

Abbreviations

AQC	Transactions of the Ars Quatuor Coronatorum
JCRFF	The Journal for the Centre of Research into Freemasonry and Fraternalism
JIVR	The Journal of the Institute of Volunteering Research
MAMR	Manchester Association for Masonic Research
THSLC	Transactions of the Historic Society of Lancashire and Cheshire
UGLE	The United Grand Lodge of England

Acknowledgements

I would like to thank a number of people and organisations who have assisted me in my research for this book; first and foremost many thanks to Fred Lomax who gave me access to the original minute book of the rebel Grand Lodge along with hidden gems such as the 1839 hand written copy of the Magna Charta and various other relics such as John Mort's Royal Arch apron and the Wigan Grand Lodge banner; Jimmy Kontzle – archivist of the Liverpool Masonic Hall in Hope Street who gave me access to the assorted correspondence and the minute book of the early rebel Committee meetings; Jim Miller, the grandson of James Miller who was the last surviving member of the Lodge of Sincerity when it was under the Wigan Grand Lodge; Diane Clements of the library and archives of the UGLE; Alec Gerrard from the Merchants Lodge in Liverpool; the reprographics department of the University of Hope, Liverpool; Richard Franklin from Arima Publishing; and friends and family for their continued support.

Foreword

This is the third book in which Dr David Harrison examines aspects of the history of English Freemasonry, and it follows on perfectly from *The Transformation of Freemasonry* which looked at the social impact that the society had on the Victorian period. This new book is about the last English rebellion in Freemasonry for over two hundred years and examines the men behind this great rift in the society, which ultimately led to the reformation of the Antients Grand Lodge.

This book takes a look at the social situation in Liverpool, discussing some of the class struggles which took place and the attempts by some to elevate themselves out of situations where there was poverty and depravation on a grand scale. This is the Dickensian backdrop to the rebellion and the formation of the Grand Lodge at Wigan.

In the early 1800s Liverpool was a thriving and rapidly expanding port; the trade in slavery and in cotton bringing wealth for Liverpool's merchants. A number of Liverpool Masonic Lodges at the time, such as the Merchants Lodge, the Mariners Lodge and the Sea Captains Lodge, had members who plied the Atlantic as both merchants and mariners and as Harrison has stated, they were actively involved in both of these central trades.

In those Liverpool lodges emerged some strong and charismatic characters who became the leaders of the rebellion against the then newly formed United Grand Lodge of England of 1813, including James Broadhurst and Michael Alexander Gage. The latter was to become famous as the leader of the rebels and this book focuses on his time in Liverpool after moving there from Kings Lynn in Norfolk. He was a very ambitious man, of that there can be no doubt, but he was also a fiery character who was not afraid to take on the might of the aristocracy of London at the head of Freemasonry at the time. Gage, a onetime tailor come surveyor, was undoubtedly behind a quite remarkable document: the 'Magna Charta of Masonic Freedom', a copy of which still exists and is included in this book.

Harrison has taken a fresh look at the circumstances surrounding this last rebellion and has given us a new insight into the mindset of the leading players. This book expands greatly our understanding of the grievances of some Freemasons in Liverpool and Wigan which led eventually to the reformation of the 'Antients' Grand Lodge later to become known as the famous Grand Lodge in Wigan which existed for ninety years.

This book I am confident will be of great interest to many brethren not just in England but overseas as well and will be a valuable addition to the library of anyone concerned with Masonic research.

I cannot recommend it too highly.

Fred Lomax
Masonic Historian and Secretary of the Wigan Association for Masonic Research

Introduction

This last English Masonic Rebellion has fascinated me ever since I first discovered about it; the skulduggery, the radicalism and the revolt that occurred within the Liverpool and Wigan lodges had me completely enthralled. I have written about the subject previously in various magazine articles and journal papers, and it was the subject for a chapter in my second book *The Transformation of Freemasonry* which was published by Arima in 2010.[1] Having since discovered new information on the rebellion, especially involving the lives of the main instigators, and in regard to the development of the Wigan Grand Lodge, it has ultimately spurred me on and influenced me to write a more comprehensive and informative book on this somewhat enigmatic story of Masonic insurrection in the early nineteenth century.

There had been a number of Masonic rebellions during the eighteenth century in England; after the 'Premier' Grand Lodge had been established in London in 1717, the Grand Lodge of All England held at York was founded in 1725, laying claim that their Grand Lodge was *'Totius Angliae'*.[2] York was an example of a localised Grand Lodge, similar to how the Wigan Grand Lodge would organise itself a century later – keeping its lodges, on the whole, within their particular county.[3] The York Grand Lodge survived until 1792, when it simply dwindled away; its remaining brethren joining the York based Union Lodge – a lodge founded by both 'Modern' and 'Antient' Masons, and, as we shall see, a number of brethren who termed themselves *'York Masons'* also joined the Lodge of Sincerity in Wigan. The 'Antient' Grand Lodge was established in 1751 in reaction to the modernisation of the 'Premier' Grand Lodge – the 'Premier' Grand Lodge being henceforth termed the 'Moderns' by the 'Antients'. Yet another Grand Lodge - the Grand Lodge of England South of

---

[1] The author has previously written on this particular subject in various articles and papers, see David Harrison, 'The Masonic Rebellion in Liverpool and the Wigan Grand Lodge', *Freemasonry Today*, Issue 30, Autumn 2004. This particular article also appeared in *Symbols and Mysteries, Freemasonry Today: The Best of 10 Years* (Lewis Masonic, 2007). The original paper was presented at the Urban History Seminar, University of Liverpool, on the 17th of March, 2004. See also David Harrison, 'James Broadhurst and the Liverpool Masonic Rebellion', in *MQ*, Grand Lodge Publications, Issue 13, April, 2005, and David Harrison, 'The Grand Lodge of Wigan: Its Rise and Fall', in *MQ*, Grand Lodge Publications, Issue 16, January, 2006. The topic was also presented as a paper by the author to the Historic Society of Lancashire and Cheshire on the 24th of March, 2010 and published in *THSLC* Vol. 160, (2012).

[2] Anon., *The Antient Constitutions of the Free and Accepted Masons, with a speech deliver'd at the Grand Lodge of York*, (London: B. Creake, 1731), p.20.

[3] The York Grand Lodge did venture into expansion much later in its existence; founding a relatively short lived lodge in Cheshire and a lodge in Lancashire. As we shall see, the Wigan Grand Lodge would have a lodge under its sway in Barnsley, Yorkshire.

the River Trent was established in 1779, when the Lodge of Antiquity – one of the oldest surviving lodges in London, rebelled against the 'Modern' Grand Lodge after a dispute, and seceded. However, this particular Grand Lodge only lasted ten years. Thus, disputes and rebellions were not uncommon within English Freemasonry, though with the union of both the 'Modern' and 'Antient' Grand Lodges in 1813, the troubles were seen to be finally over – or so it seemed![4]

With the union, there was an attempt to harmonise the ritual and ceremony, and a process of de-Christianisation within the Craft ritual took place; best exemplified with the abandonment of the Festivals of St. John in June and December. Changes also occurred within the Royal Arch ritual; seen as a fourth degree by the 'Antient's', after the union it became seen as a completion of the third degree, held in a separate Chapter room. However, this new method was not well received by some Freemasons; there was discontent against the Lodge of Reconciliation, which had been set up to smooth out the changes in the wake of the union, and the altering of the ceremonies and of the language of ritual caused alarm. Discontent in Bath occurred – resulting from friction between an Antient lodge; the Royal Sussex Lodge No. 61, and three Modern lodges. There were also disputes regarding ritual working in Bristol, along with more isolated incidents concerning particular lodges; such as the Silent Temple Lodge No. 126 in Burnley, Lancashire. In 1828, a total of 59 lodges were erased for not having made returns for a significant length of time, and no new lodges were warranted in London at all during 1813-1839.

Even the Duke of Sussex's own lodge – the Lodge of Antiquity in London, was not immune from trouble; it was no longer No. 1 on the roll after the union, having been changed to No. 2, and this upset certain brethren in the lodge. The Duke also raised criticism in his choice of appointments; for example, immediately after the union he offered the Deputy Grand Mastership to the Duke of Norfolk, and in 1838 he gave the Office of Senior Grand Warden to Lord Worsley, who had only been raised a few days before his appointment. Another close associate of the Duke's was Col. Thomas Wildman, the Provincial Grand Master of Nottinghamshire. With all the drastic changes the union brought, it was no surprise that the Duke realised that a firm hand was needed to maintain *'order, regularity and the observance of masonic duties.'*[5]

The Liverpool Masonic rebellion was the major event that not only tested the embryonic United Grand Lodge of England, but defined the end of an era - that of the 'Antients'. It was the last Masonic rebellion of its kind in England, and the story directly reflects certain important themes of the period - themes such as the defining of the class system of the early nineteenth century, not to

---

[4] See David Harrison, *The Genesis of Freemasonry*, (Hersham: Lewis Masonic, 2009), pp.179-198.

[5] See P. R. James, 'The Grand-Mastership of H.R.H. The Duke of Sussex, 1813-43', The Prestonian Lecture for 1962. For an examination of the character and life of the Duke of Sussex see Roger Fulford, *Royal Dukes*, (London: Fontana, 1973), pp.252-280.

mention the revolt and radicalism that was occurring at the time in the cotton mill towns of Lancashire. The rebellion also displays paradigms of what Dickens put forward in many of his novels of the attempts of people to climb through the social strata as the developing industrial revolution redefined issues of class.[6] Indeed, varying aspects of the very society Dickens wrote about are evident in the story of the rebellion, as are the complex interrelationships between the developing industrial towns in the north-west of England.

Overall, the Grand Lodge of Wigan also reflected a redefining of a local cultural identity during a period of social revolution, which can be mirrored in today's attempt at redefining the identities of many inner city areas in England as we embrace multi-culturalism. During the early nineteenth century, Liverpool and Wigan witnessed an increase in population that had never been seen before as Irish immigrants escaped poverty and famine, and workers migrated from around Great Britain seeking work in the industrial towns of Lancashire.

The Masonic rebellion is a story of a clash of ideas; the old and the new coming into conflict, but it can also be seen as a story displaying emerging class distinctions, reflecting the anger and frustrations of men from industrial towns who felt that they were not being listened to in a newly united society which was now dominated by a London based aristocracy. The discontent occurred in the industrial heartland of the north-west of England against a backdrop of radicalism and social unrest, and this fascinating story of the revolt, can still teach us many valuable lessons today, not just for Freemasonry, but for social issues as well. This work also celebrates the centenary of the end of the Grand Lodge of Wigan; the last remaining lodge – the Lodge of Sincerity, returning to the UGLE in 1913. The rebel Grand Lodge may have ended, but its impact resonated strongly within English Freemasonry.

---

[6] See Charles Dickens, *Great Expectations*, (Oxford: Oxford University Press, 1998), p.xii, were Pip, the leading character, is discussed as having great expectations; hoping to become a gentleman, having originated from a humble background.

Liverpool and Wigan in the early nineteenth century

Thirty or forty years ago these bells (of St. Nicholas') were rung upon the arrival of every Liverpool ship from a foreign voyage. How forcibly does this illustrate the increase of the commerce of the town! Were the same custom now observed, the bells would seldom have a chance to cease.'[7]

'...for the distance of many rods, the whole line of flagging immediately at the base of the (dock) wall, would be completely covered with inscriptions, the beggars standing over them in silence.'[8]

'...Irish deck passengers, thick as they can stand...penned in just like cattle. It was the beginning of July...and the Irish laborers were daily coming over by thousands, to help harvest the English crops.'[9]

Herman Melville, *Redburn*, writing of his experiences of a voyage to Liverpool in 1839.

The port of Liverpool in the early nineteenth century was indeed a tale of two cities; it had created immense wealth for merchants and businessmen such as the Gascoyne's, the Ewart's and the Gladstone's, but by stark contrast the port also had extreme poverty; with frequent outbreaks of disease such as cholera, typhus and scarlatina during the 1830s and 1840s, leading to the appointment of Dr. William Henry Duncan as Liverpool's first medical officer of health. The elegant Regency terraced houses of Rodney Street which housed politicians like John Gladstone, poets such as Arthur Hugh Clough and professionals such as Dr. Duncan, were in contrast to the rambling dark, dank courts that housed the sailors and dockers. Lack of sanitation and fresh water created a breeding ground for disease. The extreme poverty in the port was a breeding ground for crime.

It was a Liverpool resident - John Bellingham - who was to be the assassin of prime minister Spencer Perceval in 1812. Bellingham had pursued compensation from the British government for his imprisonment in Russia, but had had no success. Frustrated by the lack of action and feeling as though the government was not listening to his grievances; he shot the prime minister in the House of Commons. After the assassination, Bellingham had been recognised by Isaac Gascoyne who was the MP for Liverpool, Gascoyne later giving evidence for the prosecution during Bellingham's trial. Gascoyne was a Freemason, being a member of the Liverpool based Ancient Union Lodge, and

---

[7] See Herman Melville, *Redburn*, (Harmondsworth: Penguin, 1987), p.249.

[8] Ibid., p.260.

[9] Ibid., p.273.

he had been a stern supporter of the slave trade in the port, a trade which was finally abolished in 1807.

Gascoyne's argument was that by abolishing the slave trade, Liverpool's commerce would suffer, but after the abolition the port embraced new commercial opportunities and continued to increase its trade in cotton, tobacco and sugar. Liverpool also needed coal, and this produced business relationships with merchants and tradesmen from the outlining towns such as St. Helen's, Haydock and of course Wigan. Cotton was also supplied to many of these outlying areas, Liverpool's trade feeding the mighty mills of the likes of Manchester, Wigan and Warrington. Canals had been constructed such as the Sankey Canal in 1757, which brought coal from St. Helen's into Liverpool, and the Leeds and Liverpool Canal which exported cotton and other goods out of the port. The railways came in 1830, which cut the travelling time down from Liverpool to Manchester to an hour, and it wasn't long before a network of railways spread across the industrial heartland of the north-west of England, bringing the towns closer together.[10]

By the early nineteenth century, Wigan was a thriving industrial town; cotton mills and mining supplied work to both adults and children - working in harsh conditions for little pay. It was however these industries which brought the town close to Liverpool, and even before the railways, both towns were connected directly by the Leeds and Liverpool Canal, with cotton being brought into Wigan, and coal and textiles being sent out to Liverpool. Freemasonry played an important social and networking role in both Wigan and Liverpool, though not all lodges in the two towns joined the rebellion, and of those lodges that did, some were originally 'Modern' and some 'Antient'. This gives a confusing mix of ideals in support of the Masonic rebellion, but it also reveals how the discontent had spread across the traditional 'Modern' and 'Antient' divide. There were a number of Liverpool and Wigan lodges involved; some completely supporting the rebellion, others just had a number of brethren who became involved, the brethren leaving their lodge to throw in their lot with the cause. The following is a list of those lodges which had involvement; either completely or just had brethren that became drawn into the complex issues that led to the rebellion. Lodge numbers have been changed since the rebellion and

---

[10] See Owen Ashmore, *The industrial archaeology of north-west England*, (Manchester: Manchester University Press, 1982), p.20. Ashmore mentions the Leeds and Liverpool Canal as a main link between Wigan and Liverpool. See also Owen Ashmore's earlier work, *The Industrial Archaeology of Lancashire*, (Newton Abbot: David & Charles, 1969), p.114 and p.116. Ashmore discusses railway branches to various collieries including collieries in Wigan and in St. Helens, which linked them to canals. Also see Henry Tuck, *The Railway Shareholders Manuel; or practical guide to all the railways in the world*, (London: Effingham Wilson, 1848), p.105, were Tuck mentions how a colliery in Haydock is linked to the Liverpool and Manchester railway, stating the exact mileage from the port.

certain lodge names have changed,[11] thus I have used the existing or popular name of the lodge but used the original number at the time of the rebellion:

Liverpool Lodges

The Sea Captains Lodge No. 140, consecrated on the 15th of April 1765, was a vibrant lodge which had members from as far away as Boston and New York, hinting at the important Masonic trans-Atlantic links between Liverpool and ports in the USA. Other members harked from Washington, Philadelphia, Pennsylvania, Bermuda and North Carolina, while others came from Sweden and Holland. The lodge was originally a 'Modern' lodge before the union of 1813, and as the name suggests, the original members were mariners (one of the founders - Peter Humphrys - was a Sea Captain of a merchant vessel), but as time went on, local Liverpool residents joined whose occupations reflected High Street trades; such as grocers, tailors and liquor merchants such as leading Masonic rebel John Eltonhead who joined in 1817. There was also early contact between the lodge and the Wigan based Lodge of Sincerity; as a member of the Sea Captains Lodge joined Sincerity in 1801. One particular member of the Sea Captains Lodge named Samuel Woodcock, was also a member of a lodge in Rio de Janeiro, Brazil called 'The Lodge of Tranquillity', and had corresponded with the Grand Master of the rebel Grand Lodge George Woodcock (no relation), supporting the cause and his *'fight for justice'*. The Sea Captains Lodge was erased by the UGLE on the 3rd of September, 1823 and thus joined the rebel Grand Lodge outright; changing its number back to the pre-union No. 128, though it seemed to have ceased working as a functioning lodge by the early 1830s.[12]

The Mariners Lodge No. 466, consecrated on the 1st of March 1783, was also a 'Modern' lodge, and had many early members who resided around the Old Dock area of the port and, like the Sea Captains Lodge, there were both mariners and men from the High Street trades that were members; such as jeweller and leading Masonic rebel John Robert Goepel who joined in 1819. However, unlike the Sea Captains Lodge, the members during this time were mainly from Liverpool, though some mariners joined from Hull in 1816. Instead of joining the rebellion outright, the Mariners Lodge seemed to split; with a number of brethren joining the rebellion, and a number of brethren remaining, enabling the Mariners Lodge to continue as a working lodge under the UGLE. It still meets in Liverpool today. There is also a Mariners Lodge that meets in New Jersey, USA, which was founded in 1881.

---

[11] For a comprehensive examination of these English lodges and their changing numbers throughout the nineteenth century see John Lane's Masonic Records 1717-1886 online: http://freemasonry.dept.shef.ac.uk/lane/ [accessed 11th January 2012]

[12] See *Membership Lists of The Sea Captains Lodge No. 140, 1768-1836, C.D. Rom: 139 GRA/ANT/UNI, The Library and Museum of Freemasonry, UGLE, Great Queen Street, London.*

The Merchants Lodge No. 442 was consecrated on 25th of March 1780, and was a 'Modern' lodge which originally had a large number of Liverpool merchants, some of whom, like Thomas Golightlty - a founding member of the lodge, were involved in the slave trade. Other influential members included William Ewart, who was a close associate of MP John Gladstone, whose youngest son William Ewart Gladstone would later become the famous Victorian Liberal prime minister. By 1817, when the watchmaker and leading Masonic rebel James Broadhurst had joined, the makeup of the lodge had become diluted with more High Street tradesmen, and like the Mariners Lodge, a number of brethren left the lodge to join the rebel Grand Lodge, enabling the Merchants Lodge to continue working under the UGLE. It still meets in Liverpool today.[13]

The Ancient Union Lodge No. 348 was an 'Antient' lodge consecrated on the 10th of August 1792. It had boasted members of the local elite such as MP Isaac Gascoyne, and was known early on merely by its number, though according to its official history, it may have also had the name of the Mariners Lodge. Probably to save confusion with the existing Mariners Lodge in Liverpool, it was named the Union Lodge on the 19th of September 1816, and finally took on its existing name on the 16th of February 1847. The lodge had suffered a decline by 1818, and was down to ten members, but in 1820, rebels James Broadhurst, John Pilling, Arbuthnot Blain and Thomas Berry joined the Ancient Union Lodge, perhaps as a way of boosting numbers or maybe to make contacts and secure supporters for the cause. Broadhurst served as Worshipful Master, and along with Pilling, Blain, William Walker and a number of other brethren, he also joined the Mariners Lodge in 1821. Broadhurst and his followers eventually left for the rebellion, leaving the Ancient Union Lodge behind as a working lodge under the UGLE, and it still meets in Liverpool today.

Lodge No. 31, thought of itself as the leading 'Antient' lodge in Liverpool before the union, boasting the oldest Warrant, which thus gave it the right to settle disputes within the 'Antient' Masonic community of the port. It had been numbered as Lodge No. 20 before 1813, but after the union it had been renumbered to No. 31, which had caused upset amongst some of the brethren. Michael Alexander Gage had joined the lodge after moving to Liverpool and quickly established himself as a leading Freemason, serving as Worshipful Master for the lodge and taking part in Provincial Grand Lodge meetings. The lodge was central to the early part of the rebellion, and Thomas Page, an engineer aged only 25, was serving as Master during the decisive split in the lodge in 1821, which led to the expulsion of both Gage and Page and the

---

[13] See John Macnab, *History of the Merchants Lodge No. 241 1780-2004*, Revised and extended edition, (Liverpool, 2004).

ultimate erasure of the lodge by the UGLE. These events, which sent ripples of discontent through most of the Liverpool and Wigan lodges, and gathered sympathy from a handful of other lodges located farther afield, will be discussed at length later.

Lodge of Harmony No. 385 was an 'Antient' lodge that was consecrated on the 27th of December 1796. It took no part in the rebellion, but kept an eye on developments as they unfolded. During an emergency meeting which was held in 1822, a heated discussion took place with members from other lodges being present which were more directly involved in the rebellion, but the lodge continued to support the UGLE and still meets today. A later member of the Lodge of Harmony became a founding member of the Toxteth lodge No. 1356 which practises the 'Bottomley' ritual.[14]

Harmonic Lodge No. 380 was yet another 'Antient' lodge which was consecrated on the 22nd of April 1796. Not to be confused with the Lodge of Harmony above, it had been named the Lodge of Concord in 1804, before settling on its current name. This lodge did have members taking part in the rebellion such as John Eden, a Broker who was to become the first Grand Secretary of the rebel Grand Lodge, William Armstrong who was a linen draper and Azariah Santley who was a cooper. Santley had been a member of both the Mariners Lodge and the Merchants Lodge, and was active in the rebellion at an early stage, signing the 'Masonic Manifesto' on the 26th of November 1821, but he was subsequently 'restored' on the 4th of September 1822, being proposed as a subscribing member of Harmonic Lodge on the 7th of June 1823, featuring on the lodge's returns for December that year.[15] He was installed Master of the lodge on the 3rd of January 1824 – and was never again involved with the rebels. The lodge as a whole remained loyal to the UGLE and still meets today.

Wigan Lodges
Lodge of Sincerity No. 486 was a 'Modern' lodge which had been consecrated on the 30th of November 1786. It was a leading Wigan lodge, supporting the Liverpool rebels from an early stage, and was the only lodge to survive the whole rebellion; emerging to rejoin the UGLE in 1913. The make-up of the lodge was not dissimilar to the Liverpool lodges involved; mainly High Street trades being represented such as Robert Bolton who was a gunsmith,[16] grocers, various Innkeepers, and, not surprisingly, with Wigan being a mining town,

---

14 See Anon., *A History of the Lodge of Harmony No.220*, (Liverpool, 1948).

15 See *A List of the Members of the Harmonic Lodge No. 216, 1796-1836, C.D. Rom: 139 GRA/ANT/UNI, The Library and Museum of Freemasonry*, UGLE, Great Queen Street, London.

16 Robert Bolton is described as a gunsmith on his joining Sincerity on the 14th of January, 1813, and also in the 1825 Edward Baines Directory of Wigan, which lists Bolton as residing at the Market place.

some members were coal agents. No fewer than ten Masons who were termed 'York Masons' joined Sincerity from 1789-1802, such as Bookbinder John Collins who joined on the 2nd of July, 1799, and Thomas Baines, an Innkeeper who joined on the 28th of August, 1800. These 'York Masons' had actually been members of the Lodge of Antiquity – an 'Antient' Wigan lodge, but had seemingly been made welcome in a lodge which was supportive and independently minded, with Sincerity also having an 'Antient' and a 'Scottish Mason' join during the same period.[17] Despite being a leading lodge in the rebellion, the lodge was only erased by the UGLE in 1828. Sincerity took control of the reins of the rebel Grand Lodge and in its closing years, members such as John Mort became exemplary leaders. The lodge still meets today in Wigan and its story will be told in more depth later.[18]

Lodge of Integrity No. 74 was a lodge which, like Sincerity, wholly supported the rebellion. It was an 'Antient' lodge which had been consecrated on the 30th of September 1805, and like the Sincerity Lodge, Lodge No. 31 and the Sea Captains Lodge, it was completely erased by the UGLE, Integrity's erasure occurring on the 3rd of December 1823. The lodge had been numbered 54 before the union, and, like Lodge No. 31, reverted back to their original number after the rebellion. It was still in existence by the time of the reorganisation of the rebel Grand Lodge in 1838; however, it fell out with the Grand Lodge of Wigan for a while, though after reconciliation it was securely brought back into the fold. There is evidence that the lodge was still in operation in 1879, and could have survived into the 1880s.

Lodge of Antiquity, originally numbered 235, but now numbered 178, was an 'Antient' lodge consecrated on the 26th of May 1786. Ironically, as one of Wigan's oldest surviving 'Antient' lodges, it did not get involved in the rebellion, unlike the town's other 'Antient' lodge; the Lodge of Integrity. However, one of its members – William Hesketh, who was initiated into Antiquity on the 20th of February 1819, became directly involved in the Wigan Grand Lodge, becoming Master of Sincerity in 1839, and going on to serve as Junior Grand Deacon in 1840 and Senior Grand Deacon in 1842.[19] J. Brown, in mentioning the rebellion

[17] *A List of the Members of the Lodge of Sincerity No. 402, 29th of January, 1787 – 5th of September, 1821.* Pemberton Masonic Hall, Wigan. Not Listed. Also see J. Brown, *Masonry in Wigan being a brief history of the Lodge of Antiquity No. 178, Wigan, originally No. 235,* (Wigan: R. Platt, Standishgate and Millgate, 1882), p.55. Brown put forward in the history that the Lodge of Antiquity in Wigan, though an 'Antient' or 'Atholl' lodge, termed its members as 'York Masons'.

[18] See Norman Rogers, 'The Lodge of Sincerity, No. 1 of The Wigan Grand Lodge', in *AQC*, Vol. LXII, (1951), pp.33-76. The Sincerity Lodge minutes from the 21st of June 1826 to the 12th of July 1913, and membership lists are partly transcribed and discussed.

[19] See Brown, *History of the Lodge of Antiquity No. 178*, p.64. See also Norman Rogers, 'The Grand Lodge in Wigan', in *AQC*, Vol. LXI, (1950), pp.197-8. The Wigan Grand Lodge 'waste book

in his history of the lodge said that '*Antiquity took the advice of the P.G.M., and had nothing whatever to do with them*', referring to the trouble, which in his view, was caused solely by Lodge No. 31.[20]

The Barnsley Lodge

Friendly Lodge No. 557 was a lodge based in Barnsley, Yorkshire, and was to be the only lodge outside Lancashire to actively join the rebellion. It had been an 'Antient' lodge originally, having purchased its Warrant from a defunct London lodge – which was an 'Antient' method of starting a new lodge when no new Warrants could be gained. The lodge at the time of the rebellion was dominated by two local charismatic gentlemen; George Woodcock and John Staniforth Beckett. Woodcock, who was chosen as the first Grand Master of the rebel Grand Lodge, corresponded frequently with Michael Alexander Gage, and loyal support for the cause was given in 1822, though it split the lodge in two, effectively creating two Friendly Lodges working separately – friendly in name, but in regards to each other, not in nature. The brethren who stayed loyal to the UGLE continued to meet until 1827 as Lodge No. 521 (which had been the new number after the union), but, ironically, having not paid their dues to London since 1825, the lodge was officially erased in 1832. The rebel Friendly Lodge, who reverted back to their old 'Antient' number of 557, opted out of the Wigan Grand Lodge in 1827, but continued to meet until 1861 as an isolated lodge.[21]

---

minutes' from the 14th of April 1845 to the 25th of December 1857 are transcribed and discussed by Rogers.

[20] Brown, *History of the Lodge of Antiquity*, p.33.

[21] See Will Read, 'The Spurious Lodge and Chapter at Barnsley', in *AQC*, Vol. 90, (1978), pp.1-36. Read partly transcribes the correspondence and minutes of the Friendly Lodge No. 557, and discusses the history of the lodge.

Chapter 1
The beginning of the rebellion

'we deny the power of any authority to compel us to adopt a System, which has hitherto been unknown, or not practised by the ancient Masons of this Kingdom.'

Copy of the 'memorial' sent to H.R.H Prince Augustus Frederick, Duke of Sussex, read out by Michael Alexander Gage, 27th of September, 1819[22]

'My son forgot not my Law, but let thine heart keep my Commandments and remove not the Ancient Landmark which thy Father's have set.'

Michael Alexander Gage, Deputy Grand Master,
The Magna Charta of Masonic Freedom, 21st of July, 1823[23]

'you who have been the Main Instrument in Asserting and vindicating our rights in both private and public and to whom the tyrants in the Masonic world would have always looked upon with dread.'

Grand Secretary Robert Bolton writing to Michael Alexander Gage
on his resignation, 14th of June 1842[24]

On the 22nd of December 1823, a group of Masonic rebels met at the Shakespeare Tavern in Williamson Square in Liverpool to re-establish the 'Antient' Grand Lodge, a Grand Lodge that had officially merged with the 'Moderns' ten years previously. The group of Freemasons, led by a Liverpool tailor Michael Alexander Gage, were rebelling against a number of issues, but on the whole it was the adjustment to the central control of London and what they saw as the *'tyranny'* of the Duke of Sussex, who, in their eyes, had neglected their grievances concerning the ritualistic and administrative practices which had been imposed on them. The rebellion in Liverpool was the culmination of growing discontent within the large Lancashire province, which seemed to have been simmering since the union of the Antients and the Moderns in 1813.

---

[22] E.B. Beesley, *The History of the Wigan Grand Lodge*, (Leeds: Manchester Association for Masonic Research, 1920), p.5 and p.130.

[23] Ibid., p.36. This quote which appeared at the end of the 'Magna Charta of Masonic Freedom' also appeared in Laurence Dermott's *Ahiman Rezon*, (London: Robert Black, 1764), p.88. On this same page, Dermott also referred to *'the regularities of the Steward's lodge, or committee for charity, as they have been approved of and practised by the ancient York Masons in England since the year 1751'*, suggesting Dermott was aware of the practises of the York Grand Lodge.

[24] Beesley, p.86.

The Lancashire province before the rebellion was huge, and being the industrial heartland of England, was undergoing an immense increase in population as people flocked to the towns to find work. There had been a number of disputes in various Lancashire lodges since the union of 1813, such as when the Deputy Provincial Grand Master for Lancashire Daniel Lynch visited Social Lodge No. 85 - a Manchester based 'Antients' lodge. Once in the lodge room, the chair was refused to Lynch, and when one of the accompanying Provincial Officers attempted to open the lodge, the brethren refused to show the signs, saying that they *'didn't work that way...'*. The brethren also disallowed the inspection of the books. It could be said that the lodge night was overall, a very uneasy one. Other lodge disputes erupted in Lancashire, notably with lodges in Bury and Oldham during 1817; in Bury an 'Antients' lodge opposed payment of fees to the Provincial Grand Lodge.[25] In the same year, Lodge No. 545 in Todmorden on the border with Lancashire and the West Riding of Yorkshire, were said to have declared themselves 'independent' and were registering their members without submitting returns to the UGLE.[26] The general uneasiness was probably compounded by the stagnation that certain lodges were suffering at the time; some lodges like the Lodge of Lights in Warrington, the Lodge of St. John in Stockport and the Lodge of Friendship in Oldham were low on members and were also low on money.[27] Tensions over additional compulsory fees created an issue; after the union, fees were requested from all lodges for the Grand Lodge Hall fund – this of course was not very well received by certain brethren.

The Lodge of Friendship No. 519 (now No. 277) in Oldham had also witnessed internal disruption in 1817; the bickering between the brethren splitting the lodge in two. Two 'Friendship' lodges thus existed for a brief period as two halves of the lodge operated – each thinking that they were in the right, the rift only being healed the following year after the direct intervention of the Provincial Grand Master for Lancashire himself; Francis Dukinfield Astley.[28] Like the Lodge of Sincerity, the Lodge of Friendship had some members that were involved in York Masonry; the Lodge of Friendship, like Sincerity, being very open minded.[29] The Lodge of Friendship was later to write a letter to the

25 See Michael J. Spurr, 'The Liverpool Rebellion', in *AQC*, Vol. 85, (1972), pp.29-60, on p.31.

26 T.W. Hanson, *The Lodge of Probity No. 61 1738-1938*, (Halifax: Lodge of Probity, 1939), pp.231-236. Lodge No. 545 eventually returned to the fold in 1820.

27 See David Harrison, *The Transformation of Freemasonry*, (Bury-St. Edmunds: Arima, 2010), pp.59-78.

28 See *Minutes of the Lodge of Friendship, No.277, Masonic Hall, Oldham, 26th of February, 1817 – 20th of May, 1818*. Not listed. Francis Dukinfield Astley - a landowner who actually resided in Cheshire, was a poet, industrialist and had a liking for hunting and racing. His own lodge; the Lodge of Unanimity No. 89, met near his estate in Dukinfield; see John Armstrong, *A History of Freemasonry in Cheshire*, (London: Kenning, 1901), pp.263-8.

29 See *Minutes of the Lodge of Friendship, No.277, Masonic Hall, Oldham, 16th of February, 1791*, in which it is recorded that a member of the Lodge of Fortitude in Hollinwood – a lodge under the York

Liverpool rebels which was read out at a rebel Committee meeting on the 19th of November 1821, with other letters of support coming from other Lancashire lodges; such as the Lodge of Friendship No. 59 in Manchester and the Lodge of Faith No. 655 in Pilkington, both of which were read out at a previous rebel Committee meeting on the 14th of November.[30] Sympathy for the rebellion spread amongst lodges in Lancashire fairly quickly – lodges which also felt dissatisfied with the way they were being treated and identified with the Liverpool rebels. Despite the growing revolt in Liverpool, the Provincial Grand Master, Francis Dukinfield Astley, never took direct action in the port, a known hotspot which had a previous history of lodge dissent.

Disruptions in Liverpool had previously taken place in 1806, when the Grand Secretary of the 'Antient's' Grand Lodge was forced to write a letter to Lodge No. 53b which met at the Cheshire Coffee House at Old Dock Gate, after receiving a complaint - apparently from other Liverpool Antient lodges - that the lodge was open at unreasonable hours and that several members of the lodge were confined for breaking into a warehouse and stealing. The Grand Secretary requested that the lodge should suspend all Masonic business until they were cleared of the charges brought against them, but despite this request, the lodge continued to meet. The Mayor of Liverpool became involved when he received a letter from the other 'Antient' lodges of the port, and the Committee of the Masters of the Antient lodges in Liverpool started an official investigation which concluded that Lodge No. 53b had been involved in *'unmasonic behaviour'* resulting in their Warrant being withdrawn by the Antient Grand Lodge in 1807. The following year however, despite all the trouble, a number of the brethren of the erased lodge were desperately seeking a new Warrant to form a new lodge.[31]

Lancashire, as we have seen, was not the only area to be disruptive during the early part of the nineteenth century; but as a county, Gloucestershire also experienced what has been termed *'the interregum'*, due to a personal dispute between the infamous William Fitzhardinge Berkeley and the United Grand Lodge. Fitzhardinge, otherwise known as 'Bad Billy', was the eldest, but illegitimate son of the fifth Earl of Berkeley, and was a close associate of George IV, who was also a Freemason; serving as Grand Master of the 'Modern's' before the union. Fitzhardinge had a notorious reputation for being a bully, and

---

Grand Lodge, visited the Lodge of Friendship. See also Neville Barker-Cryer, *York Mysteries Revealed*, (Hersham: Neville Barker-Cryer, 2006), pp.373-4, in which Barker-Cryer explains how some members of the Lodge of Friendship also founded the Lodge of Fortitude, these members being under two Grand Lodges.

[30] Spurr, *AQC*, Vol. 85, pp.37-8. Spurr discusses and partly transcribes the various letters and the minute book of the rebel General and Committee Meetings from 26th of October, 1821 - 20th of May, 1822.

[31] *Letters concerning the Lodge at the Cheshire Coffee House, Old Dock Gate, No. 53b [erased], Liverpool Annual Returns, AR/906, 1797-1809, Library and Museum of Freemasonry, UGLE, Great Queen Street, London.*

was a rampant womaniser with a fierce, vindictive nature. He had inherited his father's estate and wealth in 1810, but being illegitimate, not the title. The Earl's death led to the infamous Berkeley Peerage Case, were the House of Lords refused to recognise Fitzhardinge as the sixth Earl after a failed attempt through forgery to prove an earlier, secret marriage between the Earl and Fitzhardinge's mother – who was reputed to be the daughter of a butcher. He had however adopted the courtesy title of Viscount Dursley, and through political influence, was later created Lord Segrave in 1831 and Earl Fitzhardinge ten years later.

Fitzhardinge was a member of the Berkeley based Royal Lodge of Faith and Friendship No. 270, and forced the lodge to petition him for the position of Provincial Grand Master for Gloucestershire in 1835, a demand which resulted in a stand-off with the United Grand Lodge. They refused to accept Fitzhardinge on the standing that only the Grand Master himself had the right in choosing the Provincial Grand Masters. Because of this stand-off, the Province of Gloucestershire had no official serving Provincial Grand Master from 1835-1856, and thus had no regular Provincial Grand Lodge, the province suffering as a result, with Freemasonry in the area declining severely. The Royal Lodge of Faith and Friendship has no records of meeting from 1851-1857, the brethren only officially meeting again the year after Fitzhardinge's death.[32]

The Liverpool rebellion however, reflected more the spirit of internal bickering and *'unmasonic behaviour'* that had resulted in the closure of Lodge No. 53b. It also mirrored the internal bickering of the Oldham based Lodge of Friendship. The rebellion was tainted with an element of isolationism and local networking 'cliques' within the lodges; some of the outlying industrial towns such as Wigan, Warrington and Ashton-in-Makerfield, had strong business links to Liverpool, mainly in relation to the cotton and coal trade, and these towns became the location for lodges which subsequently came under the sway of the rebel Grand Lodge. Many of the Liverpool lodges, like other lodges based in the neighbouring industrial towns, were also suffering from low membership and low esteem and in the acrid climate where the threat of closure and the loss of traditional rights caused increasing dissatisfaction amongst the Masons, revolt spread quickly, gaining momentum and stamina.

This period was certainly a sensitive one, and certain local lodges had their own, slightly different – almost eccentric ritual practices. Hampered by the increasing neglect of the Provincial Grand Master within the rebellious areas of Liverpool and Wigan, and with a growing feeling that their rights in the society were being eroded by the tampering of London based officials, the Liverpool rebels grew extremely sensitive during the transition era of the union. Trouble had certainly continued to simmer slowly, with further disruptions in Liverpool taking place within the Merchants Lodge, the Sea Captains Lodge, the Lodge of Harmony, and with Lodge No. 394 in Chorley, near Wigan.[33] It had been

---

[32] See C.M. Malpus, *A History of the Royal Lodge of Faith and Friendship, No. 270*, (Berkeley, 2002).

[33] Beesley, p.4.

thought that these disturbances had finally been settled by a visit from the Provincial Grand Secretary H.F. James, in the May of 1819, but it was just a sign of more serious tribulation to come.[34]

The Lancashire Masonic rebels were mainly a collective of Liverpool and Wigan based tradesmen, and, under the leadership of the tempestuous Michael Alexander Gage, these rebels created innovative documents which can be seen as radical social statements of the time; such as the 'Masonic Manifesto', the 'Unalterable Determination' and the groundbreaking 'Magna Charta of Masonic Freedom'. With this resolve, the rebels went on to successfully re-establish the *Grand Lodge of Free and Accepted Masons of England According to the Old Constitutions, granted by His Royal Highness Prince Edwin of York, Anno Domini Nine Hundred twenty and six*, in 1823, which later became known as the *Grand Lodge held at Wigan*.[35] The rebels directly referred to the York Legend in their title; a tradition championed by the York Grand Lodge that, in the year 926, Prince Edwin had founded the first Grand Lodge at York. This early gathering of Masons had supposedly adopted certain Constitutions, which the rebel Grand Lodge title also referred to. The 'Antients' Grand Lodge had also respected this legend, and it was not uncommon for some 'Antient' lodges to feature the Edwin legend in their warrant.[36] The 'Magna Charta of Masonic Freedom' was such a bold and sensationalist statement for the period, the majority of which was probably written by the turbulent Gage himself; the very fiery and radical nature of the document seething with Gage's rhetoric, the power of its wording asserting a new direction for Freemasonry – a direction which took the society away from the union. It reflected the rebels' grievances and outlined their hope for an independent future, but it also reflected Gage's outright rebellious personality; the document discussing the *'Despotic Authority'* and *'the Love of Absolute Power'* that the United Grand Lodge had practiced.[37] It was Gage's unfaltering leadership and his organisational expertise that set him up as a 'founding father' of the re-launch of 'Antient' Freemasonry.

---

[34] See the copied minutes of the Provincial Grand Lodge of Lancashire 1818-1825, Liverpool Masonic Hall, Hope Street, Liverpool. Not listed.

[35] The word *'Constitutions'* in the title was sometimes replaced by *'Institutions'* in certain early minutes from 1823-1825, and the word *'Ancient'* was also inserted into the title at various points. *The Grand Lodge held at Wigan* has also been referred to as the *The Grand Lodge in Wigan* and the *Wigan Grand Lodge* by various historians.

[36] For the York Legend see Kenneth Mackenzie, *The Royal Masonic Cyclopaedia*, (Wellingborough: The Antiquarian Press, 1987), p.180 and p.774. Edwin has also been identified with the Northumbrian king who laid the foundation stone of York Cathedral, in about 626. See also Harrison, *Genesis of Freemasonry*, p.182. The Wigan based Lodge of Antiquity – an 'Antient' lodge, featured the Edwin legend in their warrant; see Brown, *History of the Lodge of Antiquity No. 178*, pp.16-17.

[37] Beesley, p.26 and p.31.

Ironically, many of the leading Liverpool based Masonic rebels were originally from outside the port, such as Gage, who was born in Norfolk, James Broadhurst, a watchmaker from Great Sankey near Warrington and John Robert Goepel, a Jeweller who originated from London. A study of these leaders presents a fascinating insight into their character and how the rebellion managed to take hold so quickly.

Michael Alexander Gage: The early career of the Masonic Rebel

Michael Alexander Gage was born in 1788 in Kings Lynn, Norfolk, and, like fellow rebels James Broadhurst and John Robert Goepel, he had migrated to Liverpool, lured by the business opportunities that the rapidly expanding port presented. He had left Kings Lynn in the summer of 1811 and seems to have spent some time in Scotland before settling in Liverpool; becoming a member of Montrose Lodge No. 70 on the 19th of September, 1811, and an Honorary Member of the Patrick Kilwinning Lodge in Glasgow a few days later on the 24th of September. He certainly found Freemasonry as an entrance into local society, and as he moved from port to port, Gage sought out local lodges to join. Gage only appears in Liverpool by the December of 1812, with the first record of him occupying the 1st Principal's Chair on the 20th of that month, when incidentally there was a disturbance in the Chapter, perhaps an inclination of things to come! [38] He settled in Liverpool quickly and had married Sarah Browne in the October of 1816 at St. Anne's Church,[39] establishing himself as a tailor and as a leading Mason of Lodge No. 31.[40]

Gage had been a petitioner for the 'Antient' Philanthropic Lodge while at Kings Lynn, and became the first Worshipful Master of the lodge on the 14th of May, 1810.[41] He was successful at gaining his old lodge's *'co-operation'* during the early stages of the rebellion, a co-operation which certainly added confidence to the rebels as it would have given them hope of expanding their influence, and, it would have undoubtedly helped to maintain Gage's high standing within the rebel group. It was his recollections of this lodge that inspired his suggestions to rebel Grand Master George Woodcock concerning the correct 'Antient' regalia to wear in office, something he mentioned in a letter to Woodcock on the 8th of December 1825. Gage put forward that the exact mode of dress was *'Grand Officers: A white lamb skin Badge lined and edged with Purple silk - Purple strings with gold tassels, and the emblem of their office embroidered in Gold in the centre of the Badge with Purple Sashes and Gold Jewels. N.B. the Grand Master only is allowed to have any other device upon his Badge, which is generally made of White Satin, with Armorial Bearings of the*

---

[38] See Rogers, 'The Grand Lodge in Wigan', *AQC*, Vol. LXI, pp.196-7.

[39] Liverpool Mercury, 1st of November, 1816, issue 279, p.7.

[40] See Gore's Directory of Liverpool for 1825, (Liverpool: Gore & Sons, 1825), p.111, which lists Gage as a tailor residing at 10, Fleet Street, Liverpool.

[41] See Hamon Le Strange, *The History of Freemasonry in Norfolk 1724-1895*, (Norwich: Agas H. Goose, 1896), p.207 and p.216.

Ancient Fraternity richly emblazoned theron and which Ornament is strictly applicable to the dignity of his high office.' This style of apron was worn throughout the existence of the Grand Lodge of Wigan by the Grand Master.[42]

In the same letter, Gage also enclosed a *'Draft of the Past Master's Jewel which (was) copied from the one presented to me by the Ancients Lodge at Lymm (Kings Lynn) of which I was the Father previous to the Union.'* This jewel, having been worn by Woodcock at his lodge meetings, still exists, bearing a Sheffield hallmark from 1826, and is owned by the current Friendly Lodge No. 1513. The description of the regalia had been presented almost word-for-word by Gage at a rebel Grand Lodge meeting in June 1825, making it clear that the dress code was strict and distinct.[43]

Early hints of discord in Gage's life begin to appear when he was declared Bankrupt on 17th of November, 1821, during the very time he was instigating the Masonic rebellion. His dire financial situation which had been exposed to the public, may have certainly added to his anger and frustration, Gage's actions gaining more force from this point, perhaps with him spending so much time on Masonic matters his business suffered as a result.[44] The bankruptcy was certainly a hint of things to come in his later life.

James Broadhurst: naval hero, watchmaker and Masonic Rebel

James Broadhurst was baptised on the 25th of August, 1771, at St. Mary's Church, Great Sankey. He was the son of a watchmaker, and James followed in his father's footsteps, eventually moving to Liverpool, where he set himself up as a watchmaker and married Christian Litherland at St. Nicholas' Church in Liverpool in 1794. Christian was the younger sister of the renowned Liverpool watchmaker Peter Litherland, who had also originated from Warrington, and was famous for inventing the patent lever watch. Litherland had relocated to Liverpool in 1790, and James developed a close relationship with the fellow watchmaking family. With the outbreak of the French wars, Liverpool was rife with press gangs, but in 1795, with the passing of the Quota Acts, Liverpool had to find 1,711 men for Naval service; men who would volunteer for service in return for payment of a 'bounty'. Broadhurst was 'inrolled' into the Navy in April 1795; being recently married with a child on the way, he may have been attracted by the 'bounty' offered for volunteering, but it was certainly akin to the 'impressment' for a newly married watchmaker whose first child was to be born a month later. He was posted to HMS Namur, taking part in the decisive Battle

---

[42] See the picture of John Mort's apron.

[43] Beesley, pp.52-56. See also Read, *AQC*, Vol. 90, p.16.

[44] See George Elwick, *The Bankrupt Directory: The Complete Register of all the Bankrupts with their residences, trades and dates when they appeared in the London Gazette, from December 1820 - April 1843*, (London: Simpkin, Marshall and Company, 1843), p.154. See also the Liverpool Mercury, 23rd of November, 1821, issue 547, p.7.

of Cape St. Vincent on the 14th of February 1797, which was an outstanding victory for the British, revealing the brilliance of Nelson.[45]

He had progressed from Landsman to Ordinary Seaman, and finally to Able Seaman, and on the 28th of December, 1800, Broadhurst was transferred to the *San Josef,* one of the two captured Spanish ships from the battle, which displayed Nelson's flag for a time in early 1801. It would be another two years before Broadhurst was released from service, and on doing so he returned to his family in Liverpool and to watchmaking. He was later to receive the Naval General Service medal in 1847, the medal only being presented to the veterans still surviving at the time.[46] In 1817, like many veterans of the Napoleonic Wars, he entered into Freemasonry, joining the Merchants Lodge, and in 1820 he joined the Ancient Union Lodge where he was to serve as Worshipful Master. Both of these lodges included members that became actively involved in the rebellion,[47] and Broadhurst, being older and having served on the *San Josef* when Nelson had hoisted his flag on the ship, would have been seen as a naval hero, giving him a respect which would have made him an obvious leading figure in the rebellion.[48]

Broadhurst took an active part in the Provincial Grand Lodge meetings, and was quick to join his fellow Masonic tradesmen in the rebellion, sharing the same grievances, freely giving his signature to the documents which outlined these issues. The discontent had developed a year after Broadhurst had become a Freemason and had quickly gathered pace, and as the joining of other Liverpool lodges became prevalent during the this period, he would have met many of the rebels such as John Eltonhead and John Robert Goepel. Perhaps,

---

[45] *Family papers of James Broadhurst.* Private collection. Not listed. See also Macnab, *History of the Merchants Lodge,* p.161 and Nicholas Rogers, *The Press Gang: Naval Impressment and Its Opponents in Georgian Britain,* (London: Continuum International Publishing Group, 2007), pp.113-114, in which Rogers discusses how 'enrolment' into the Navy by press gangs took place.

[46] See Gore's Directory of Liverpool for 1825, (Liverpool: Gore & Sons, 1825), p.59, which lists Broadhurst as a watchmaker residing at 4, Trowbridge Place, Liverpool. See also the 1841 Census for Liverpool, Lancashire. Liverpool Library, Ref: HO107/561/15, indicating Broadhurst was still working as a watchmaker, aged 69.

[47] *Family papers of James Broadhurst.* Private collection. Not listed. See also *Minutes of the Ancient Union Lodge no. 203, 1795-1835,* Garston Masonic Hall, Liverpool. Not Listed, and Macnab, *History of the Merchants Lodge,* p.141.

[48] Nelson hoisted his flag on the *San Josef* in January, 1801, after arriving at Plymouth, but transferred his flag to the *St. George* less than a month later. The respect for able seamen who had served under Nelson is displayed in early nineteenth century literature, such as in *Redburn* by Herman Melville. *Redburn* was based on Melville's own visit to Liverpool in 1839, and in the book, on arriving in Liverpool docks, a description of the '*Dock-Wall Beggars*' is given. The sailors walking past the beggars ignored them, except for one; '*an old man-of-war's man, who had lost his leg at the battle of Trafalgar*', his wooden leg being made from the oak timbers of the *Victory*. This beggar was respected by the sailors and '*plenty of pennies were tost into his poor-box*' by them. See Herman Melville, *Redburn,* (Middlesex: Penguin, 1987), p.261. A reference to the status of being a naval hero is also made in Charles Dickens's *David Copperfield,* by Mr. Micawber, a character who is down on his luck but who is also honest. Micawber describes himself as '*a gallant and eminent naval Hero*'; see Charles Dickens, *David Copperfield,* (New York: Sheldon and Company, 1863), p.138.

like his fellow tradesmen, after surviving through the Napoleonic Wars and hardships of the early decades of the nineteenth century, Broadhurst sought equality and freedom of speech, which was perhaps the initial attraction to a society which he felt held those qualities.

John Eltonhead: Liquor merchant and landlord of the Castle Inn[49]

John Eltonhead was born in Liverpool in 1780, and worked as a liquor merchant. He had joined the Sea Captains Lodge in 1817 as a joining member from the Merchants Lodge; a lodge which he continued to play an acting role in during 1817 and 1818, when he served as Treasurer.[50] He would have known James Broadhurst quite well, as Broadhurst served as Senior Warden in the Merchants Lodge during 1818, and he would have also brushed shoulders with other rebels from the Merchants Lodge such as Samuel Money Blogg and Azariah Santley. Eltonhead then served as Worshipful Master of the Sea Captains Lodge, and like Gage and Broadhurst, took a leading role early on in the rebellion, the Castle Inn being vital as the location of the early meetings of the rebels.

Indeed, the rebels conducted their energy fuelled Committee meetings in the Masonic Rooms there, and used the Castle Inn as their correspondence address, duly electing Eltonhead as their Treasurer on the 26th of November, 1821, a role which he embraced. At the same General meeting, the rebels had sent a letter to all lodges interested in helping, asking them to subscribe £1.00 each. Eltonhead thus had the responsibility for these funds as the donations came in, such as the £1.00 which they received from the Lodge of Faith on the 18th of March, 1822.[51] Eltonhead became a staunch member of the rebel Committee, co-signing a number of letters and documents such as the 'Masonic Manifesto' and the 'Unalterable Determination', and had put his signature to a letter complaining about the conduct of the Provincial Grand Master after the inquiry meeting on the 6th of August, 1821.[52]

---

[49] Liverpool Mercury, 25th of April, 1823, issue 621, p.5, and Liverpool Mercury, 16th of May 1823, issue 624, p.4, both of which state in the Sales by Auction section that '*A well accustomed Inn, known by the name of the Castle Inn North, situated on the West side of Scotland Road, now in the occupation of Mr John Eltonhead, with good stabling for 7-8 horses and rooms over.*' Also in the Liverpool Mercury, 4th of November, 1825, issue 754, p.7, which recorded the death on the 29th of October 1825 of the '*much and deservedly respected Mrs. Mary Kirby age 67, widow of the late Thomas Kirby, and mother of John Eltonhead, Castle Inn North*'. Family papers of John Eltonhead. Private collection. Not listed.

[50] See *Membership Lists of The Sea Captains Lodge No. 140, 1768-1836, C.D. Rom: 139 GRA/ANT/UNI, The Library and Museum of Freemasonry, UGLE, Great Queen Street, London.* See also John Macnab, *History of the Merchants Lodge No. 241 1780-2004*, Revised and extended edition, (Liverpool, 2004), p.141 and p.185.

[51] See the transcribed collected letters and minutes of the Liverpool rebel Committee, from 26th of October, 1821 - 20th of May, 1822. Liverpool Masonic Hall, Hope Street. Not listed.

[52] Ibid.

Eltonhead had also been a member of the charitable Free and Easy Society of Mersey Street in Liverpool, serving as its President in 1816, gaining plenty experience of the leadership of local societies.[53] However, like Gage, in August, 1817 Eltonhead had also suffered bankruptcy,[54] though he was managing the Castle Inn by 1821 which came up for sale in the April of 1823, just as the rebels were about to re-launch the 'Antient' Grand Lodge. He was expelled by the UGLE along with the likes of Gage and Goepel, but never appeared to have served as an Officer in the rebel Grand Lodge. Eltonhead was again in trouble in 1824, appearing at Lancaster Castle as an Insolvent Debtor,[55] but he continued to work at the Castle Inn until the following year, when he drastically altered his profession to a '*car owner*'.[56] However, Eltonhead found himself back in the Lancaster Court House in July 1829,[57] and he died on the 18th of May, 1835, aged only 55.[58] It seemed to have all gone wrong for Eltonhead, something that was also mirrored in other rebel's lives.

John Robert Goepel: Jeweller and Masonic Rebel

John Robert Goepel was born in London on the 30th of August, 1797, and baptised on the 18th of December the same year. He moved to Liverpool and worked as a '*jeweller and chaser*',[59] marrying Rosamond Ward at St. James' Church on the 20th of December, 1821, just as the Masonic rebellion was picking up pace. He had only joined the Mariners Lodge in 1819, but he threw in his lot with the rebels almost immediately, attending the Committee meetings at the Castle Inn, adding his signature to the 'Masonic Manifesto' and the 'Unalterable Declaration' and, along with Gage, Eltonhead and Thomas Page, Goepel was

---

[53] Liverpool Mercury, 27th of December, 1816, issue 287, p.1.

[54] The London Gazette, 5th of August, 1817, issue 17274, p.1717; The Times, 6th of August, 1817, issue 10217, p.2, and the Liverpool Mercury, 12th of September, 1817, issue 325, p.8. See also 'The European Magazine and London Review Containing a Monthly List of Bankrupts', Vol.72, from July to December 1817, (London: printed for James Asperne, 1817), p.183, and 'The New Monthly Magazine and Universal Register', Vol. VIII, from July to December 1817, (London: H. Colburn, 1817), p.182. Also The London Gazette, 13th of April, 1819, issue 17468, p.667.

[55] The London Gazette, 23rd of March, 1824, issue 18012, p.495. Eltonhead was listed as an 'Innkeeper'.

[56] See Gore's Directory of Liverpool for 1825, (Liverpool: Gore & Sons, 1825), p.101, which lists Eltonhead as residing at the Castle Inn North, New Scotland Road, Liverpool, and Gore's Directory of Liverpool for 1827, (Liverpool: Gore & Sons, 1827), p.113, which lists Eltonhead as a '*car owner*' residing at 4, Ellenborough Street, Liverpool.

[57] The London Gazette, 7th of July, 1829, issue 18591, p.1290. Appearing at the Lancaster Court House, Eltonhead was listed as being '*formerly of New Scotland-Road, Victualler and Car-Proprietor, and late of Ellenborough-Street, Liverpool.*'

[58] Liverpool Mercury, 22nd of May, 1835, issue 1255, p.7, death '*in the 55th year of his age, Mr John Eltonhead, formerly of the Castle Inn North, Scotland-road.*'

[59] See Gore's Directory of Liverpool for 1825, (Liverpool: Gore & Sons, 1825), p.117, which lists Goepel as residing at 13, Bevington Street, Liverpool.

one of the diehard group of rebels expelled from the UGLE on the 5th of March, 1823.

Despite his expulsion, he never appeared on the list of Grand Officers during the subsequent rebel Grand Lodge meetings, being conspicuous by his absence. His most senior position in the Mariners Lodge had been Senior Warden in 1822, and he may have taken a back seat in the rebel Grand Lodge affairs, choosing to work in Gage's Lodge No. 31 after the break with the UGLE.

The road to Rebellion

The trigger for the rebellion started at a Provincial Grand Lodge meeting held at Ye Spread Eagle Inn, Hanging Ditch, Manchester, on the 12th of October, 1818, a motion was proposed by Michael Alexander Gage from Lodge No. 31, and was seconded by the Master of the Sea Captains Lodge, which declared that *'when any lodge hereafter be reduced to any number of Members less than seven, they ought not to be considered as a regular Lodge, and consequently their Warrant should be declared void, and its number be placed at the disposal of the United Grand Lodge.'* This motion, which was a move to correct a defect in the 1815 *Book of Constitutions*, was carried by an overwhelming majority. The motion was then duly passed on to the Board of General Purposes, but instead of it being presented by them to the United Grand Lodge, the Board declared that is was best not to stray from *'that silence on the subject which had been observed in all the Books of Constitution'*. Certain Liverpool lodges, such as the Ancient Union Lodge, an old 'Antient' lodge which had experienced some trouble in the past with Lodge No. 31, only had ten members at the time, and the lodge had held an emergency meeting prior to the Provincial Grand Lodge meeting, sending a brother to attend, keeping an eye on the proceedings.[60]

Many lodges at this time, especially in the industrial areas of Lancashire, had suffered a decline in the wake of the Unlawful Societies Act of 1799. Freemasonry had suffered stagnation in the province of Lancashire, and only a few new lodges had been founded in the area during the early decades of the nineteenth century.[61] The majority of the Liverpool lodges, some suffering more than others from low attendance, bonded together; the low attendance leading some Freemasons to join other lodges, such as when Broadhurst and some other brethren from the Merchants Lodge - who were to play an important role in the rebellion - joined the Ancient Union Lodge, a move which

---

[60] Beesley, pp.2-4. See also Spurr, *AQC*, Vol. 85, p.31.

[61] A somewhat rare example of a surviving lodge that emerged during this stagnant period was the Blackburn based Lodge of Perseverance No. 345, constituted in 1815, a lodge that certainly lived up to its name.

ensured not only the survival of the struggling lodge, but would have created greater bonding between the brethren.[62]

Almost a year later at a Provincial Grand Lodge meeting in Liverpool on the 27th of September, 1819, it was proposed by Gage that a 'memorial' should be submitted which he had prepared,[63] addressed to the Grand Master himself – the Duke of Sussex, which would thus outline the grievances of Gage and his supporters; focussing on the fact that the motion which had been passed during the meeting the previous year had not been presented by the Board of General Purposes to the United Grand Lodge. The 'memorial' to the Duke was approved during the meeting; it was signed accordingly by the Provincial Grand Lodge Officers and was despatched to the Duke. The 'memorial' also put forward how Lancashire brethren – because of the great distance from London, could not attend Grand Lodge and vote on matters which concerned them, and also referred to an incident in Bath, where Petitions for Royal Arch Chapters had been dismissed by the Grand Chapter because it was *'not desirable to make the Number of Chapters in any place equal to the Number of Lodges'*.[64]

Gage seized upon this example, and, being of 'Antient' persuasion, he indicated that they saw the Royal Arch as part of Craft Masonry, and the rejection of the Petitions was an abuse of power. The Duke of Sussex however, did not reply to the 'memorial'. Indeed, the Masonic historian Beesley puts forward that the original 'memorial' may have been seen as troublesome and was thus destroyed, though a copy does exist in the United Grand Lodge Library.[65] The Duke was extremely dismissive of any disagreeable elements within Freemasonry and had little sympathy for rebels within the society. Such was the case with the outspoken Freemason Dr. George Oliver, whose removal from his Provincial office was engineered by the Duke after Oliver incurred his dislike.[66] The 'memorial' had certainly been quite direct and revealed the anger felt by Gage and his supporters, complaining how certain 'Modern' practices were being enforced and how new rules concerning the Royal Arch conflicted with the *'Ancient Landmarks'*.

Having received no reply only intensified the anger of the Gage and his followers, but the very fact that they had actually instigated contact with the Duke using such contemptuous language also ignited the anger of other certain

---

[62] *A List of the Members of the Ancient Union Lodge No. 203, 1792-1887, Harmonic Lodge No. 216, 1796-1836, & St. George's Lodge of Harmony No. 32, 1786-1836, C.D. Rom: 139 GRA/ANT/UNI, The Library and Museum of Freemasonry, UGLE, Great Queen Street, London.*

[63] Beesley, pp.4-5.

[64] A Copy of the Address to His Royal Highness Prince Augustus Frederick, The Duke of Sussex, Grand Master of the United Grand Lodge of Ancient Free and Accepted Masons of England, transcribed in Beesley, p.132.

[65] Beesley, p.5.

[66] R.S.E. Sandbach, *Priest and Freemason: The Life of George Oliver*, (Northamptonshire: The Aquarian Press, 1988), p.99.

individuals; at another Provincial Grand Lodge meeting held in Preston on the 9th of October, 1820, James Spence of the Liverpool based St. George's Lodge, viciously attacked the 'memorial', brutally criticising the language used. The Deputy Provincial Grand Master Daniel Lynch – who had initially supported the 'memorial', now turned heel and supported Spence, and despite an eloquent speech made by Gage in support of the issues raised in the 'memorial', a vote was taken and the 'memorial' was officially withdrawn, Gage had lost the day with seventy three in favour of withdrawing the 'memorial' to thirty five against. This decision culminated in Gage and his followers seeking extra support from Liverpool lodges, but there was also a faction against Gage's actions within his own lodge causing it to split in two.[67]

The opposition to Gage in his lodge was led by Henry Lucas and James Greetham, and it appears that the lodge was a hotbed for heated disputes and arguments. In a lodge meeting on the 18th of October 1820, the Master had reported on the events of the previous Provincial Grand Lodge meeting, and it was stated that the 'memorial' to the Duke had not even been discussed or placed before the lodge for approval anyway. Gage contradicted this and stated that it had – although there was no mention of it in the minutes. At the next meeting on the 1st of November, on arriving at the lodge room at Freemasons Hall in Bold Street, they found it was already in use, and the brethren were told that *'it was inconvenient to find us all accommodation for the future'*. They found another room to hold the lodge, and after the previous minutes were read and confirmed, James Greetham contradicted Gage's previous statement by saying that the 'memorial' had never been submitted for approval in the lodge before the Provincial Grand Lodge meeting in 1819. The trouble got steadily worse, and in a meeting of Lodge No. 31 on the 15th of November, Gage made an official complaint against Lucas, who had lodged a staggering twenty four charges against Gage before the Board of General Purposes, none of which incidentally had been previously put before the lodge for discussion. It was moved that the lodge should not get involved in a personal quarrel between the two brethren, and the Board of General Purposes also came to the same conclusion later on. However, the gloves were off between Gage and Lucas, and the ensuing fight would destroy the peace and harmony of the lodge forever.[68]

In a lodge meeting held on the 7th of March, 1821, Thomas Page was about to take the Chair and open the lodge, being the current Master, when he was suddenly interrupted by Greetham who presented him with a letter which he insisted was to be read out before the lodge was opened. Page told him that if the letter was on the subject of Masonry then it would be read during open

---

[67] See Spurr, *AQC*, Vol. 85, p.32 and Rogers, 'The Grand Lodge in Wigan', *AQC*, Vol. LXI, p.174. See also Beesley, pp.5-7.

[68] Spurr, *AQC*, Vol. 85, p.33.

lodge, at which point Greetham abruptly declared that the lodge was suspended and that the letter was actually a copy of the suspension, which he persisted in reading himself. Greetham – as Senior Warden, then refused to take his chair, so Page requested another Brother to take the position. As he tried to open the lodge, Lucas, Greetham and their supporters *'in a most insulting and indecorous manner immediately divested themselves of their badges (aprons), cast them upon the floor and afterwards kicked and trampled upon them'*. They declared that they did not have to obey Page as Master as they were not in a lodge, and *'used any possible means in their power to prevent the Worshipful Master from opening the Lodge by laughing, talking and walking about the room during the ceremony of opening the Lodge.'* They were aided in this rather childish act by a number of other followers, and it seemed that the whole event had been premeditated to cause maximum disruption.[69]

Despite the deliberate distractions, the lodge was eventually opened, and Lucas and his followers withdrew themselves from the room *'in a most contemptuous manner'*, Page going on to read Greetham's letter, which commented on the *'alarming dissention and gross irregularity in the proceedings of the said Lodge and Chapter, whereby harmony is destroyed and the Fraternity in general much scandalised'*. It appeared that Lucas and his followers had asked for the suspension themselves, and Provincial Grand Master Dukinfield Astley had responded, writing the letter and granting the suspension. The lodge thus split in half; with Gage and Page leading one half, and Lucas and Greetham leading the other, though Gage and his followers from the lodge still held meetings in defiance of the suspension, and sent a string of letters in protest to the Provincial Grand Master. In a letter to the Provincial Grand Lodge dated the 28th of May, 1821, Gage and his followers stated that they refused to enter into negotiations until Greetham had restored the property of the lodge.[70]

What had started as a feud between two men had escalated and was spiralling out of control; Gage and his followers were openly defying the suspension, Greetham broke open the lodge chest, taking the jewels, the silverware and the working tools, claiming he had the authority of the Provincial Grand Master, and as other lodges began to be drawn into the dispute, Liverpool Freemasonry edged ever closer to a full blown revolt. On the 8th of June, a letter was received by Lodge No. 31 from the Provincial Grand Lodge, which stated that the Provincial Grand Master *'judges it expedient to remove, and does hereby remove the said suspension'*, thus leaving the door open for an inquiry. Gage and his followers however, wrote back defiantly stating that they would face the charges made against them as long as they were given a copy of those charges and were faced by their accusers.[71]

---

[69] Ibid.

[70] Ibid., p.34. See also the transcribed collected letters and minutes of the Liverpool rebel Committee, from 26th of October, 1821 - 20th of May, 1822. Liverpool Masonic Hall, Hope Street. Not listed.

[71] Ibid.

By this time though, trouble was spreading; when the Mariners Lodge had expressed sympathy with the plight of Gage and his followers, it also had its lodge chest broken open by two of its members, removing the Warrant. To make matters worse for the rebels, the man chosen as Chairman of the Committee to inquire into the dispute of Lodge No. 31 was none other than the Deputy Grand Master Daniel Lynch – the same person who had supported the withdrawal of the 'memorial' to the Duke of Sussex. When the inquiry began on the 6th of August, 1821, problems erupted immediately as James Spence – the member of St. George's Lodge, who had originally proposed the withdrawal of the 'memorial' to Sussex, raised an objection to the presence of a representative of the Ancient Union Lodge – Thomas Berry. This objection was duly put to the vote, but on seeing that the majority was against him, Lynch suddenly closed the meeting, took off his Masonic regalia and ordered that the books of Lodge No. 31 should be locked up again.[72]

This disastrous end to the inquiry further sparked the powder keg of revolt, bringing a number of disgruntled Liverpool brethren from various lodges together in disgust. They assembled at John Eltonhead's Castle Inn, North Liverpool, and with open support coming from the Liverpool based Mariners Lodge, the Ancient Union Lodge, the Sea Captains Lodge and the Merchants Lodge, Gage and the rebels quickly organised themselves and formed a Committee, from which they could focus on gaining a wider support base, not just in Lancashire, but beyond. They began meeting regularly – their first meeting being on the 26th of October, 1821, and they took no time at all in launching an attack on those they saw responsible for their unjust treatment, namely Lucas, Greetham and Lynch.[73]

For example, at a General meeting on the 14th of November, 1821, the rebels resolved that a letter should be sent to the Provincial Grand Master, which attacked Lucas and Greatham, describing them as *notorious disturbers of the Fraternity*, but they saved their most vitriol language for Lynch, who, they stated, had *identified himself with those disorderly Brethren who have committed the scandalous outrages which have disgraced the name of Masonry in this Town and consequently a most unfit person to have the absolute power of deciding upon the merits of a case of so much importance to the interests of the Fraternity*. Lynch had certainly invoked the anger of the rebels, and they charged him *with exercising a gross and impolitic partiality to men whose conduct has most decidly met the general disapprobation of the Craft in this Town*.[74]

The rebels were building up to a decisive meeting on the 26th of November, after they had invited representatives from Lancashire lodges to attend on that date. At a Committee meeting on the 19th of November, the rebels decided that Lynch and Spence (along with a few others), who could actually attend the

---

[72] Ibid., pp.34-5.

[73] Ibid.

[74] Ibid., p.38.

meeting – were to be prohibited from entering as it was '*highly derogatory to the dignity of the intended Meeting to allow such persons to sit amongst its body*'. The likelihood of Lynch and Spence coming to the meeting was of course extremely remote.[75]

The decisive General meeting at the Castle Inn, North Liverpool, held on the 26th of November, 1821, at 9 o'clock in the morning, set the final scene for rebellion. A 'Masonic Manifesto' was drafted with 34 signatures, including Gage, Broadhurst, Eltonhead and Goepel, outlining the unjust treatment dealt by the UGLE on the rebels. The printed document, which also displayed the events leading up to the suspension of Lodge No. 31, was sent out to all lodges under the UGLE. Broadhurst was the Master of the Ancient Union Lodge in 1821, and along with a number of brethren including Thomas Berry, they represented their lodge, duly adding their signatures to the Castle Inn document. Representatives from Broadhurst's original lodge; the Merchants Lodge, included tailor Daniel Mackay and excise man Samuel Money Blogg. The Sea Captains lodge was represented, amongst others, by the landlord of the Castle Inn John Eltonhead, and the Mariners Lodge by Azariah Santley and John Robert Goepel.[76]

The document was printed and subsequently posted to all lodges, and reaction was swift; the Duke of Sussex, who was serving as Master of the London based Lodge of Antiquity No.2, received a copy, and on the 5th of December, he wrote to the Provincial Grand Master of Lancashire Dukinfield Astley, instructing him to find out whether the persons who were shown as signatories to the document had given their sanction to its publication. Of course, if any brethren had knowingly put their signature to a printed or published document concerning the proceedings of any lodge, or had named the persons present without the direction of the Grand Master or the Provincial Grand Master, under Section 6 of the 1815 *Book of Constitutions*, they would be suspended immediately. Thus all 34 rebels were duly suspended.[77]

At a rebel meeting on the 31st of December 1821, they were all aware of their suspension, and when the Committee met at the Castle Inn on the 21st of January, 1822, they put forward a new document as their 'Unalterable Determination' which had the additional signatures of nine members from the Lodge of Integrity and twelve from the Lodge of Sincerity – the Wigan Masons had now gotten directly involved. A further boost came with a letter of support that had arrived from none other than Thomas Harper, who had been a member of the Lodge of Reconciliation; Harper reassuring the rebels that '*Had our illustrious Brother the Duke of Kent (that truly Ancient Mason) been alive he would I am sure have stood forward to advocate your cause; but I trust your appeal will have the effect of*

---

[75] Ibid.

[76] Ibid., pp.37-9.

[77] Ibid., p.39.

raising many champions and that you will succeed in your praise worthy and honourable attempt to uphold the Ancient land Marks.' During the early part of 1822, letters of support arrived from various Lancashire lodges, but one in particular arrived from a Yorkshire lodge; the Friendly Lodge in Barnsley, being signed by Past Master George Woodcock, a man destined to play a greater role in the rebels' grand plan.[78]

The Duke of Sussex was at this time however, still willing to review the whole situation. Although Lancashire was in the northwest of the country, far removed from the cultivation and culture of London, the county was undergoing a rapid industrial transition and its population was vastly increasing. Radicalism and revolt was commonplace in the mill towns of Lancashire with the Peterloo Massacre still being very fresh in the minds of worker, mill owner and aristocrat, and letting the rebels take hold of Freemasonry in the county could prove extremely damaging for the union which was still in its infancy. Sussex reacted and suspended Dukinfield Astley and his deputy Daniel Lynch on the 7th of March, 1822, to the delight of the rebels, and after Thomas Page had written to Sussex asking for their lodge books to be restored to them in able to prepare their defence, the Grand Master had stated that the books of Lodge No. 31 should be returned to the rebels as long as they were handed back for the next quarterly communication.[79] It seemed as though the rebels could be reconciled, but the Duke of Sussex had underestimated their determination in resurrecting the 'Antient' Grand Lodge.

---

[78] Ibid., p.40. For information on Thomas Harper , his life, his work in Freemasonry and his family, see Richard J. Reece, 'Thomas Harper', in *AQC*, Vol. 84, (1971), pp.177-186.
[79] Spurr, *AQC*, Vol. 85, p.41.

A print of Nelson receiving the sword from the Spanish Admiral aboard the *San Josef* after the battle of Cape St. Vincent in 1797. Masonic Rebel James Broadhurst served on the ship which, for a brief period in 1801, was Nelson's flagship.

'We of the Enlightened Men...' a photo of the Masonic certificate of James Broadhurst who joined the Liverpool based Merchants Lodge in 1817.

TO

ELIAS JOSEPH, ESQ. TREASURER,

And the rest of the Proprietors,

THIS VIEW OF THE FREE MASONS' HALL,

WHERE THE ROYAL ARCH LODGE, NO. 20, IS HELD,

SITUATE IN BOLD-STREET,

IS HUMBLY DEDICATED, BY THEIR OBLIGED SERVANT,

T. TROUGHTON.

A print of the Masonic Hall which was based in Bold Street, Liverpool. Lodge No. 31 met there before being erased by the United Grand Lodge of England.

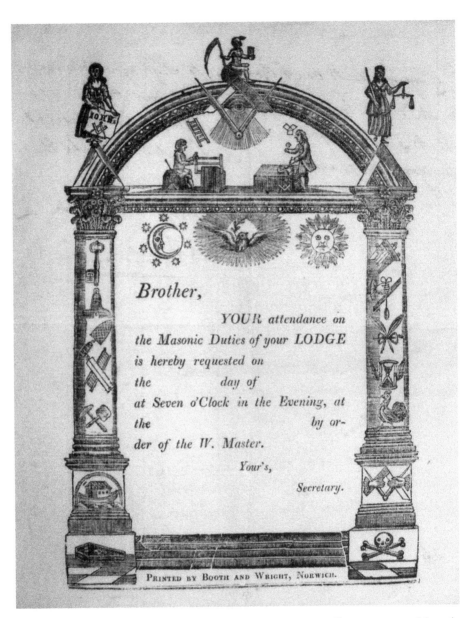

A lodge summons from the early nineteenth century, revealing numerous Masonic symbols such as the sun, the moon, the skull and crossbones and the set square and compasses. Written on the back was a note to 'Br Gage' asking him to sign his name 'on the fine lines in the margin of your Grand H.R.A Certificate'.

A collection of rebel names from the first Rebel Committee minute book, including Thomas Page, Michael Alexander Gage, John Robert Goepel and James Broadhurst, during a General meeting held on the 14th of November, 1821.

MANIFESTO

'...*having hitherto been frustrated by arbitrary unpolitic, and unmasonic power*' - a photo of a page from the first Rebel Committee minute book showing the faded writing of the Masonic Manifesto from the 26th of November, 1821.

COPY *of the* ADDRESS

To His Royal Highness — Prince August Frederic
Duke of Sussex,
Earl of Inverness, Baron Arklow, Knight
Companion of the Most Noble Order of the
Garter
and
Grand Master
Of the United Grand Lodge of Ancient
Free and accepted Masons of England.

Most Worshipful & Royal Sir,
We, the deputy Provincial Grand Master [and]
(having the other officers & members of the Provincial)
Grand Lodge of the County of Lancaster, [...]

The copy of the beginning of the address to the Duke of Sussex, taken from the first Rebel Committee minute book.

At the top of the same page as the beginning of the address to Sussex are listed 34 names that signed the Masonic Manifesto, including Gage, John Eltonhead, Broadhurst and Goepel.

of Constitution we have invariably [...]
with the Rules laid down therein for our
guidance in this respect; but finding [...]
all our attempts towards this end frustrated
we were left to the only alternative (viz:) that
of applying to every branch of the [...] Grand
Lodge through the medium of a Printed [...]
cular, or, [...] submit to innovations [...]
abuses unparalleled in the annals of
Masonry —

Hence arised our indignation at the attempt
to cast an odium upon us, for discharging
our Masonic duty:

We therefore wish it to be understood that
we shall not rest satisfied until full and
perfect justice be administered without reference
to rank or station; nor will we suffer our
rightful privileges to be curtailed or the
Ancient Land Marks of Masonry to be
removed and this is our **UNALTERABLE**
DETERMINATION.

Thomas Page   W.M. 31

Michael Alexr Gage   P.M.

Thomas Fagan   J.W.

Joseph Martin   Treasurer

John Smith   Secretary

Peter Forrest   P. Secretary

Elias Owens   S.D.

John Boyard

Thomas Bullock   W.M. 74

Thomas Peers   S.W.

John Molyneux   J.W.

The Unalterable Determination from the first Rebel Committee minute book, dated from the 21st of January, 1822. Gage's signature can be seen under that of Thomas Page.

Some other signatories of the Unalterable Determination, showing Goepel and Broadhurst. Eltonhead had also signed as Past Master of the Sea Captain's Lodge above, and selected brethren of Integrity and Sincerity from Wigan also signed on another page.

Chapter 2
The rebel Grand Lodge in Liverpool

'The patience and fortitude that we have displayed under the most insults and the scandalous outrages, seem only to have prepared the way for further injury...'

Copy of a letter from Lodge No. 31 to the Provincial Grand Master,
30th of August, 1821.[80]

'This Magna Charta of Masonic Freedom shall be intrusted to the care and keeping of the Grand Master for the time being, who shall at his installation renew the solemn engagement herein contained, and promise to deliver this Instrument to his Successor after Legal nomination Election and Installation according to Ancient Custom.'

Landmark No. 16 of the Magna Charta of Masonic Freedom,
21st of July, 1823.[81]

'This extraordinary and insufferable conduct caused the Secession of several Lodges and many individual Brethren, upon the incontrovertible grounds that the Articles of Masonic Union having been violated, the Contract was thereby broken, and the Covenant was thereby dissolved, hence it follows that the United Grand Lodge of Ancient Free and Accepted Masons of England has by inevitable consequence ceased to exist.'

The Magna Charta of Masonic Freedom,
21st of July, 1823.[82]

On hearing that Lodge No.31 had continued to meet, the lodge was callously and unceremoniously erased after a unanimous vote at a United Grand Lodge meeting on the 5th of June, 1822, an action that mirrored the erasing of Lodge No.53b in 1807. This action created further isolation for the suspended rebels as they were not allowed to visit any other lodges, ultimately providing greater bonding between the rebels and giving them further cause to complain about the *'tyranny'* of the United Grand Lodge. The dissent spread rapidly through Liverpool and Wigan as lodges began to throw in their lot with the outcasts. In May 1823, the Liverpool based Sea Captains Lodge threatened to separate itself entirely from the UGLE if Lodge No. 31 was not re-instated, and thus the Sea

---

[80] The transcribed collected letters and minutes of the Liverpool rebel Committee, from 26th of October, 1821 - 20th of May, 1822, pp.28-32. Liverpool Masonic Hall, Hope Street. Not listed.

[81] See Beesley, p.36.

[82] Ibid., p.27.

Captains Lodge was also hastily erased in September, along with Integrity from Wigan. This seemed to be the point of no return.

Local 'Antient' lodge politics certainly added to the tensions in Liverpool; Gage's Lodge No. 31 had been the 'senior' lodge amongst the 'Antient' lodges in Liverpool, having the oldest Warrant, and therefore having the position to settle the disputes that occurred within other 'Antient' lodges within the town. The lodge had been called Lodge No. 20 before the union, but had been subsequently re-numbered, and, in doing so, had lost some of its local prestige. This re-numbering was obviously a sore point for the lodge as they swiftly reverted back to No. 20 on the creation of the rebel Grand Lodge in 1823. The Warrant for Lodge No. 20 had been purchased by a number of brethren from the Ancient Union Lodge shortly after the lodge had been founded in 1792, and, with the purchase of this Warrant which dated from 1753, these brethren left the Ancient Union Lodge and founded Lodge No. 20, which instantly became the oldest 'Antient' lodge operating in Liverpool; out-dating and thus displacing the local St. George's Lodge, which, despite being founded in 1786, had a Warrant which only dated from 1755.[83] St. George's Lodge became extremely aggressive in its attitude to the rebels, particular against the conduct of Gage and his followers from Lodge No. 31, and, when looking at the membership makeup of the St. George's Lodge, a greater number of local gentlemen and merchants are evident, such as James Spence who was a merchant, whereas in Lodge No. 31, the membership makeup had a greater number of tradesmen, such as Gage who was a tailor. There were clear issues of class within the dispute, and this may explain the anger felt by Gage - a man with high aspirations.[84]

These social issues were something that the enemies of Gage and the rebels were clearly aware of; a satirical poem which was anonymously published entitled '*Longstitch*', characterised Michael Alexander Gage as '*Mighty Alexander Longstitch*' who was described as a '*poor Tailor, who for got to "cut his coat according to his cloth"*'. The poem's references to class were strikingly obvious, and Gage was mockingly portrayed as '*enlisting*' men for his cause – as a '*recruiting sergeant*', but the ambiguity of the word '*list*' which was used in the poem, was also scornfully referred to as '*the selvege of woollen cloth...often used by little boys for garters.*' Masonic references were littered throughout the piece, such as Gage being described as '*P.M. of The Shopboard*' and that '*Longstitch might as well have been Longneedle or Landmark as Longsword.*' The poem parodies Gage as a tailor fighting against the Duke of Sussex and sarcastically mocks his lower status:

---

[83] St. George's Lodge of Harmony No. 32 had been No. 25c, changing to No. 38 in 1814. It was renumbered again to No. 35 in 1832, and changed to its present number in 1863. See Lane's Masonic Records 1717-1894 online: http://freemasonry.dept.shef.ac.uk/lane/ [accessed 11th of January, 2012]

[84] Many thanks for the work of Joshua Civin, Merton College, Oxford, who had previously examined the makeup of the Liverpool lodges during the rebellion period.

'A Knight of the Thimble being a well known designation or appellation of that industrious class of men (or fractional parts of men.)'

The piece was a disgusting attack on the class and status of Gage and his fellow rebels; it was obviously written by someone with knowledge of Gage and the rebellion in Liverpool, and with knowledge of Freemasonry. The society prided itself on representing equality and freedom, but this poem was an example of the issues of class which not only divided English Freemasonry at the time, but also English society, issues which clearly lay behind the rebellion.[85]

Other lodges now had to decide if they were going to stay with the UGLE or fully join the rebellion, leading to heated debates. One such meeting was held at the Lodge of Harmony on the 2nd of December, 1822, at the Magpie and Stump in Key Street, Liverpool. The Lodge of Harmony, like the Ancient Union Lodge and Lodge No. 31, had belonged to the 'Antient' Grand Lodge before the union. This lively meeting had visitors from The Merchant, Mariners, and Ancient Union Lodges, all Liverpool lodges which had certain members directly involved in the rebellion. This particular period certainly revealed a lodge in crisis as the Worshipful Master and Wardens were appointed during an emergency meeting and not elected or installed as was the custom. The members were very much aware of the irregularity concerning the situation of the Lodge of Harmony as *'it was the opinion of the members present that a letter should be sent to the Grand Lodge to know the present state of this Lodge'*. It seems that the lodge was letting the UGLE know of their position during this time of upheaval in Liverpool. Despite this show of loyalty, the Worshipful Master that had actually been elected in 1822 was suspended two years later for twelve months, for what is described as *'unmasonic conduct'* and another brother was suspended for seven years.[86]

On the 5th of March, 1823, the United Grand Lodge finally expelled 26 brethren, stating that the rebels had:

'been found guilty of various Acts of insubordination against the Authority of the Grand Lodge, and having been summoned to show cause why they should not therefore be expelled from the Craft; have not sent any sufficient apology for their late misconduct'.

Their rebellious activities were described as an *'insult'* by the United Grand Lodge and the brethren, having *'violated the laws of the Craft'*, were ostracized. The list of the 26 expelled brethren revealed the usual suspects; including Gage, Page, Eltonhead, Goepel, Berry, various leading brethren from Integrity and Sincerity, and a certain David Watson from the Royal Lancashire Lodge No. 182

---

[85] Anon., *Mighty Alexander Longstitch by Simon Sap, and his friend Snap.* UGLE: Provincial Correspondence Files 4/Miscellaneous Printed Material.

[86] See Anon., *A History of the Lodge of Harmony No.220,* (Liverpool, 1948), pp.7-8.

in Colne.[87] This action however played directly into the hands of the rebels, and Gage and his followers were now free to proceed with their master-plan – to resurrect the 'Antient' Grand Lodge. The plan was certainly to go national and to spread the influence of the rebel Grand Lodge; this is clear when it was declared during their first rebel Grand Lodge meeting that the causes which led to the re-establishment of the 'Antient's' were to be advertised in four of the London Papers, a public declaration which would be guaranteed to reach the eyes of the 'tyrannous' leaders of the United Grand Lodge.[88]

Gage, though being the spiritual leader of the rebellion, took on the role of Deputy Grand Master, while George Woodcock Esq. was duly elected as the Grand Master of the Rebel Grand Lodge. Woodcock was the renowned member of the Barnsley based Friendly Lodge and fully supported the '*Antient landmarks of Freemasonry*'. He was in correspondence with Gage and the rebels in Liverpool from early 1823, Woodcock putting forward an eight part resolution which outlined the '*sorrow and regret at these severe measures which the G. Lodge has thought it proper to exercise towards Twenty-six respectable members of the Society*'.[89] Woodcock struck up a long-distance friendship with Gage, both being very like-minded, with the new Grand Master seeking advice from his Deputy on numerous occasions in regard to the administration of the rebel Grand Lodge and issues relating to the Royal Arch.

The new Grand Master was listed as a *Gentleman* in the minutes of his lodge meetings, but he worked as a bank manager for a fellow member of the lodge; John Staniforth Beckett – a member of a local banking family. Despite this, Woodcock appears to have been in control of the lodge and certainly engineered the lodge in joining the rebellion; a decision that ultimately split his lodge in two, mirroring the incident which had occurred at the Lodge of Friendship in Oldham and Lodge No. 31 in Liverpool. Indeed two Friendly Lodges existed for a while, but Woodcock and his supporters had taken possession of the Warrant and the tools, enabling their rebel lodge to claim legitimacy in their actions. Woodcock certainly shared the same spirit as his fellow rebels in Liverpool and Wigan, though events were soon to dampen the flaming fire of revolt.

The rebel Grand Lodge was quickly organised, and after the inaugural meeting on the 21st of July, 1823, the minute book begins with the celebratory meeting at the Shakespeare Tavern, Williamson Square on the 22nd of December, where the 'Magna Charta of Masonic Freedom' was read out and ratified.[90] Gage was in the Chair as he was serving as Master of Lodge No. 31

---

[87] Beesley, pp.16-19. The list of brethren can also be found as a circular pasted into the membership lists of the Mariners Lodge.

[88] Ibid., pp.39-41.

[89] Read, *AQC*, Vol. 90, p.10.

[90] Beesley, p.41.

(re-numbered 20), and present at this special meeting was a certain Ian Somerville, a representative from Lodge No. 212 under the Grand Lodge of Scotland, and Thomas Strong, a representative from Lodge No. 548 in Ireland.[91] Their presence was no accident, as Gage, in re-launching the 'Antient' Grand Lodge, wanted the Grand Lodges of Scotland and Ireland to be fully aware of the move, perhaps in an early attempt to get endorsement for the rebels. Somerville and Strong also signed the Magna Charta, and though Woodcock did not attend, he *'was thrice proclaimed Grand Master of Masons'*, and it was declared that *'the thanks of this meeting be given to Brother George Woodcock for the firmness with which he has supported the cause of Ancient Freemasonry, and for the Honor done to the Craft by his Accepting the Office of Grand Master under such manifest inconvenience to himself.'* Woodcock was then installed Grand Master by proxy *'according to ancient custom.'* Woodcock had given his permission for his name to be used in the *'Public Papers as Grand Master'* and the Grand Officers were installed; the Officers being a mixture of both Liverpool and Wigan brethren.[92]

The new Grand Lodge then began to meet regularly; their next meeting being held in Wigan on the 1st of March, 1824, with Gage presiding as Grand Master *'Pro Tempore'* over a collective of Wigan Grand Officers. However, the rebels suddenly experienced an unexpected crisis. At the next meeting of the Grand Lodge which was held at the Cross Keys in Wigan on the 23rd of June, it was resolved unanimously by the Wigan Grand Officers that the Liverpool based ex-Grand Secretary John Eden was *'for ever expelled…in consequence of his having Embezzled the funds of the Grand Lodge for his contempt of Summonses and other unmasonic conduct.'*[93] Eden had joined Gage's lodge when the rebel Grand Lodge had been founded, and this would have been a personal blow to the spiritual rebel leader – on top of which it would have created difficulties for the financial status in the early days of the rebel Grand Lodge, presenting obvious trust issues and embarrassment, especially for the Liverpool brethren. Part of the Grand Secretary's job would have been to assist in looking after funds, and Eden had certainly abused the trust that had been placed in him. The returns paid to the Grand Secretary from certain lodges under the sway of the new rebel Grand Lodge had not been passed on to the Grand Treasurer, Eden fraudulently using the funds. It seems that this incident had certainly shaken the fledgling rebel Grand Lodge, affecting the brethren deeply, some of whom became quickly disenchanted. Gage was notably absent from this meeting.

During the same year, James Broadhurst turned his back on the rebellion and conformed. Broadhurst, who was never expelled and was not evident at the meeting at the Shakespeare Tavern in December, 1823, presented an apology to the United Grand Lodge, which brought him back into the fold. He

---

[91] Ibid, pp.36-9.

[92] Ibid., pp.39-40.

[93] Ibid., pp.46-7.

immediately rejoined his original lodge - the Merchants Lodge, but his payments ceased in 1826, the experience of the rebellion and the subsequent fall-out perhaps affecting the camaraderie of the lodge. Broadhurst continued to work in Liverpool as a watchmaker, and died in October 1851, being buried at the Wesleyan Brunswick Chapel in Liverpool. Out of the original rebels representing the Ancient Union Lodge, Thomas Berry remained to play an active part in the rebel Grand Lodge. Berry had joined Gage's Lodge after being expelled by the UGLE; he had attended the decisive meeting at the Shakespeare Tavern and went on to serve as Grand Secretary in the March meeting of 1825.[94]

The Grand Lodge met yet again in Wigan on the 15th of December, and it was noted that present at this meeting were *'The Grand Officers resident in Wigan'*,[95] suggesting that there were separate appointed Grand Officers for when the Grand Lodge met in Wigan and separate appointed Grand Officers for meetings in Liverpool. Indeed, at the same meeting that Eden was expelled, the Wigan brethren had replaced him with John Thacker – a member of Sincerity, who was thus one of their own brethren.[96] The Grand Lodge met again in Wigan on Christmas Day to celebrate St. John's Day, and George Woodcock – who was again not in attendance, was declared *'Elected Grand Master of Ancient Masons for the ensuing year'*. Gage was also not in attendance, and again, the Officers were made up of Wigan brethren. Gage however, was conveyed a *'vote of thanks in pure Masonic Form'*, and was to later sign all the individual minutes for the meetings that year. It appeared peace and harmony had been restored after a troubled first year.[97]

However, financial trouble persisted, and in 1825, it was again discussed at a Grand Lodge meeting held at *'the house of Brother William Jorden Suffolk Street'* in Liverpool on the 6th of June, that the Barnsley Lodge returns had not been passed on by the Grand Secretary to the Treasurer. Although the Grand Secretary in question was not named; Thomas Berry had taken on the role at the last meeting on the 7th of March, which had also been held in Suffolk Street, Liverpool, and he was conspicuous by his absence during the June meeting. This new incident, coming so soon after the Eden affair, sent alarm bells ringing throughout the rebel lodges, even though it appears from the minutes that it was down to negligence rather than the outright embezzlement as before. It was also noted in the meeting that the *'Lodges in Wigan were Three Quarters in arrear...'* and *'it was resolved that in consequence of this negligence and apparent contempt manifested by*

---

[94] Ibid., p.39 and p.51.

[95] Ibid., p.47.

[96] See the membership lists of Sincerity in Rogers, 'The Lodge of Sincerity, No. 1 of The Wigan Grand Lodge', in *AQC*, Vol. LXII, p.61 and p.64. John Thacker joined Sincerity on the 22nd of June, 1796, aged 21; his occupation was a *'Fustian maker'*. A John Thacker also signed the bye-laws in 1820.

[97] Beesley, pp.49-50.

the Grand Secretary and the Lodges in Wigan, that the D.G. Master should be requested to Write to the said Lodges and also to the Grand Secretary in his Official Capacity...'[98]

It is evident that there was some growing tension between the Liverpool and Wigan brethren, perhaps even some rivalry and distrust; the Grand Lodge had been meeting in Wigan throughout 1824 with mainly Wigan Officers, but an uneasy and fragile balance seems to have been maintained with the Grand Lodge gathering in Liverpool for the two recorded meetings in 1825. However, the June gathering was the last recorded meeting of the rebel Grand Lodge until 1838, and the irregularities caused by the Grand Secretary seemed to have generated further discord in the harmony of the brethren. A proposed Grand Lodge meeting in Manchester never materialised, and George Woodcock's Barnsley Lodge became dismayed at the continued financial irregularities occurring in the administration of the rebel Grand Lodge, and, after some deliberation, formally separated themselves from their Lancashire brethren in the April of 1827, Woodcock resigning his office of Grand Master.[99]

The correspondence between Gage and Woodcock ended soon after, and in a letter to Woodcock dated June 1828, Gage declined meeting Woodcock and the brethren of the Barnsley lodge in Manchester, and also declined an invitation by Woodcock to spend Christmas at Barnsley. Gage also outlined in the letter how he had been putting Masonry before business for too long, and that he must now start devoting himself to concentrate on his *'plan of Liverpool'*.[100] The Barnsley lodge – being the only Yorkshire lodge in support of the rebellion – thus styled themselves as *'The Yorkshire Lodge of Ancient Masons'*, and Woodcock continued to lead his lodge in isolation until his death in 1842.[101]

There seems to have been a split between the Wigan and Liverpool brethren; a deep schism created by distrust and suspicion. There were a number of leading Liverpool rebels who had left the new Grand Lodge around this time, either by choice or expulsion; Broadhurst had gone, Eden had been expelled in disgrace, Berry no longer appeared in the minutes ever again, and even Gage – the spiritual leader of the rebellion, was to distance himself. It was if the Liverpool brethren were becoming acutely disillusioned with the new Grand Lodge, their energy and enthusiasm quickly ebbing away. Perhaps if these Liverpool brethren had stayed with the rebels, the rebel Grand Lodge may have continued to meet occasionally in Liverpool, and not, as we shall see, have moved permanently to Wigan. With the financial irregularities occurring at the hands of two Grand Secretaries and ever growing suspicion – the Liverpool, Wigan and Barnsley lodges seemed to have become disenchanted with the way the Grand Lodge was being organised, and time was needed to heal the wounds.

---

[98] Ibid., pp.52-3.

[99] Read, *AQC*, Vol. 90, pp.16-17.

[100] Ibid., p.26 and p.31.

[101] Ibid., p.23.

Chapter 3
The Wigan Grand Lodge

'...having hitherto been frustrated by arbitrary unpolitic, and unmasonic power'

The Masonic Manifesto,
26th of November, 1821.[102]

'...we are now more than ever convinced that the unprecedented mode of proceedings adopted towards Lodge No: 31 is intended as a prelude to the utter annihilation of the inherent privileges of every Warranted Lodge upon record; for the express purpose of establishing a Monstrous and insufferable Arbitrary power.'

The Unalterable Determination,
21st of January, 1822.[103]

'The Grand Secretary's fee be five shillings for Writing Magna Charta to be paid by the Lodge it is for.'

Robert Bolton being charged to re-write the Magna Charta of Masonic Freedom during a Wigan Grand Lodge meeting, 23rd of December, 1839.[104]

The Masonic Rebellion in Liverpool as we have seen, had included from its early stages a number of Wigan lodges, and after June 1825, no minutes exist of the Grand Lodge ever meeting in Liverpool again, though in Gage's resignation letter written in 1842, he stated that he had *'not had the pleasure of meeting the Grand Lodge, nor in fact any private Lodge during the last fifteen years'*, which indicates that he may have continued to attend his own lodge or perhaps an ad-hoc Grand Lodge meeting for another two years at least.[105] Indeed, in a reference in the minutes of the Lodge of Sincerity dated the 12th of December, 1827, Gage is referred to as *'Grand Master of Liverpool'*, and on the 28th of February, 1832, the Sincerity minutes declare that a representative was appointed *'to meet Br. Gage of Liverpool for the purpose of forming a Union through the County.'* The industrious intention of the Wigan brethren was to get the Grand Lodge organised again, and on the 10th of July the following year, there was reference to the agreement made between the rebels over eleven years previously in the 'Unalterable Determination'; *'and*

---

[102] The transcribed collected letters and minutes of the Liverpool rebel Committee, from 26th of October, 1821 - 20th of May, 1822, pp.21-22. Liverpool Masonic Hall, Hope Street. Not listed.

[103] Ibid., pp.36-9.

[104] See Beesley, p.72.

[105] An excerpt from Michael Alexander Gage's resignation letter, 10th of June, 1842, transcribed in Beesley, p.85.

that Unalterable determination is that they shall give Lodge 31 of Liverpool a fare Investigation.' It seemed that the Wigan brethren were determined to re-establish the Grand Lodge – with or without 'Grand Master' Gage.[106]

The makeup of the Liverpool and Wigan lodges that were involved in the rebellion were strikingly similar; with the majority being tradesmen and all sharing the same grievances, but the shift from Liverpool to Wigan was to become a permanent one. Another leading Liverpool rebel, John Eltonhead, had returned to the United Grand Lodge on the 7th of March, 1827,[107] the same year that Gage had stated that he had last attended a lodge. With these two leading rebels gone, it left only a handful of active Liverpool brethren, such as Thomas Page and John Robert Goepel, to mix with an influx of leading Wigan rebels, such as William Hesketh, John Burrows and Robert Bolton.

Despite the abolition of slavery in 1807, the port of Liverpool continued to grow as merchants and investors found new trade and new business. William Ewart, the Liverpool broker and a leading member of the Merchants Lodge, became a founder of the Committee to support the proposition of the building of the Liverpool and Manchester railway.[108] On the 15th of September, 1830, the Liverpool and Manchester railway was finally opened by erstwhile Freemason the Duke of Wellington, an event attended by an array of local dignitaries, and connected the port, not only to the cotton producing town of Manchester, but the whole of the industrial north-west of England, bringing the area closer together, cutting down the transport time between Liverpool and Manchester to an hour.

The railway also brought social and business networking closer together, and especially aided the cotton, coal and iron making industries in the area.[109] The northwest of England soon became criss-crossed by interlinking railways and within a few years of the opening of the Liverpool to Manchester railway, the cotton and coal producing town of Wigan became connected, this new easy transport bringing the Masonic rebels closer together. Indeed, it was not long after the introduction of the railways that the Masonic rebels moved their centre of operations to Wigan, though the Liverpool brethren could still be found in attendance, an example being seen in the membership lists of the Lodge of Sincerity, which mentions a Liverpool timber merchant called Richard Green joining in 1831.[110] The rebellion in Liverpool had struck a blow to Freemasonry in the port, and it would be the mid-nineteenth century before the society would

---

[106] Rogers, 'The Lodge of Sincerity, No. 1 of The Wigan Grand Lodge', in *AQC*, Vol. LXII, p.43.

[107] Spurr, *AQC*, Vol. 85, p.42.

[108] John Macnab, *History of The Merchants Lodge, No. 241, Liverpool, 1780-2004*, Second Edition, (Liverpool, 2004), p.34.

[109] 'The Manchester and Liverpool Rail-Road' in the *Monthly Supplement of The Penny Magazine of The Society for the Diffusion of Useful Knowledge, March 31 to April 30, 1833*, pp.1-3.

[110] See Rogers, 'The Lodge of Sincerity, No. 1 of The Wigan Grand Lodge', *AQC*, Vol. LXII, p.65.

start to expand. However, the newly constructed Western Division of the Province of Lancashire – formed in 1826 to make the large county more manageable - soon made its presence known within Liverpool, and prominent local figures such as Robertson Gladstone were appearing in the membership list of the St. George's Lodge – especially as the lodge could now claim to be the oldest surviving 'Antient' lodge in the area.[111]

There is a large gap in the main minute book from the last known meeting in Liverpool in June 1825, until the 13th of April 1838, when the Grand Lodge suddenly resumed its meetings in Wigan at the Hole I'th' Wall tavern in the Market Place. Gage was notably not in attendance, but original rebels Thomas Page, from Lodge No. 31, (renumbered to its original pre-union number of 20 after the rebellion) and Robert Bolton, from the Lodge of Sincerity, were involved. A new local Grand Master; William Farrimond Esq. was elected, officially replacing the long gone George Woodcock, who had never actually attended the Grand Lodge meetings anyway, and the rebel Grand Lodge began a new phase as it took on more of a Wigan identity, gradually severing its ties with Liverpool. The Sea Captains Lodge had ceased to exist by the early 1830s, so, with only one Liverpool based rebel lodge working, it made more sense to re-locate permanently to Wigan, which was a more central location within Lancashire, had more rebel lodges operating, and was more determined in re-establishing the Grand Lodge.

The new Grand Master William Farrimond Esq. was listed as a Yeoman from Pemberton when he joined the Lodge of Sincerity on the 1st of April, 1819. He was only 26 on his initiation, and was involved in the rebellion from the start; and, although he was not on the list of expelled brethren in 1823, his social standing as a local 'Squire' made him an obvious choice to be elected as Grand Master in 1838, a position he served until 1847.[112] Farrimond was listed as a farmer on the 1841 census, and was retired by 1861, but in the village of Pemberton, which lay on the outskirts of Wigan, he would have been seen as a gentleman farmer, living a fairly affluent lifestyle.[113]

After the significant meeting in April 1838, the Wigan Grand Lodge meetings took place regularly, meeting almost every quarter in various Wigan taverns, some of which were run by its own Freemasons; such as the Hole I'th' Wall which was run by Brother Thomas Johnson; the Bankes's Arms, which was run

---

[111] *List of Members for Lodge No. 35 held at the Adelphi Hotel – Liverpool, December 18th, 1839.* Liverpool Masonic Hall, Hope Street, Liverpool. Not listed.

[112] See Rogers, 'The Lodge of Sincerity, No. 1 of The Wigan Grand Lodge', *AQC*, Vol. LXII, p.64.

[113] *William Farrimond, yeoman of Pemberton; lease of messuage called Green's House and closes in Pemberton, 2nd of October, 1790,* Ref: E (B) 1438, Ellesmere (Brackley) collection. Also see 1861 Census for Pemberton; William Farrimond, aged 67, was residing at Lower Harry House, Clap Gate Lane, as a '*Retired Farmer*', with his wife Martha, his daughter and two granddaughters. Wigan Library, Wigan; Ref: RG 9/2782.

by Brother Thomas Bolton; and the Angel Inn in nearby Ashton-in-Makerfield, which was run by Brother Timothy Turton.[114] Wigan was well placed in the centre of industrial Lancashire, and at its height in the early 1840s, the Wigan Grand Lodge had lodges under its sway in Wigan, Liverpool, Ashton-in-Makerfield, Warrington, Ashton-under-Lyne, and had also re-established contact with the lodge in Barnsley and an old 'Antient' lodge in Kings Lynn, Norfolk, which was probably Gage's old Philanthropic Lodge.

This new meeting of the Wigan Grand Lodge in April 1838 personified a progressive cornucopia of concepts; apart from electing a new local Grand Master, they organised a procession through Wigan to celebrate Queen Victoria's coronation. This became a very public display for the newly reborn Grand Lodge; a banner was designed, the Committee being requested '*to purchase 60 yards Mazarine Blue Ribbon 3 ½ inches broad.*'[115] The banner still survives and reveals an array of Masonic symbols such as the sun and the crescent moon, along with the square and compass' and the level – all surrounding the declaration that this was The 'Antient' Grand Lodge.[116] The Wigan Grand Lodge certainly used the more enigmatic symbols of Freemasonry, such as when they painted the Grand Lodge cupboard with the 'All seeing eye' above the legend '*The Grand Lodge of Ancient Free and Accepted Masons of England*', similar to the banner.[117] The coronation procession was also advertised in the *Wigan Gazette*, sending a direct message out to other lodges in the Wigan area that came under the UGLE that the rebel Grand Lodge was functioning, organized, and was taking a leading part in the town's procession. It was an example of civic pride and represented a new dawn for the Grand Lodge; a Grand Lodge that was to become more culturally embedded with Wigan. The procession took place on Thursday the 28th of June, 1838, after which they dined together at the Commercial Hall.[118]

The Barnsley Lodge however, had ultimately decided not to celebrate Victoria's coronation at Wigan, having turned down the invite to join the Wigan Grand Lodge in the procession. A letter sent to the Wigan brethren stated rather bluntly that '...*We esteem all permanent Grand Lodges as an hindrance to the free exercise of Ancient Freemasonry as they are always attended with great expense and no adequate benefit returned.*' The letter went on '*We look upon a permanent Grand Lodge as an incubus upon the Craft, continually causing uneasiness instead of that healing power which it pretends to have...*' The memory of the money problems which had almost

---

[114] Timothy Turton is mentioned in the 1861 Census for Ashton-in-Makerfield as a '*Retired Publican*', aged 70, Wigan Library, Wigan; Ref: RG 9/2786.

[115] Beesley, p.57.

[116] See the photo of the Wigan Grand Lodge banner.

[117] Beesley, p.73.

[118] A reproduction of the advertisement was presented in Beesley, p.144, and can be seen as a photograph in this book taken from the main minute book.

caused the rebels to disintegrate over ten years before was still fermenting with the Barnsley brethren, and they were keeping a steady distance from the new revamped Wigan Grand Lodge.[119]

The Barnsley brethren had previously declined to take part in a procession through Barnsley in celebration of the coronation of William IV in September 1831; George Woodcock had put the matter forward in an emergency lodge meeting '...*to take into consideration the propriety or not of walking in (the) procession.*' One of the brethren – Brother Locke, had proposed that they should walk, but John Staniforth Beckett moved '*That we, as Freemasons cannot with propriety join the public procession to celebrate the King's Coronation on the 8th inst., because that ceremony has reference to political matters, between which and Freemasonry there is not, nor ever ought to be, any sort of communication whatsoever...*' The Barnsley lodge was now making up its own rules, but, as not to appear unpatriotic and totally rebellious, Beckett's amendment added '*...Nevertheless we do hereby declare our loyal attachment to the Sovereign of our Native Land, as dutiful Masons ought to do.*' Beckett's amendment was seconded and the Barnsley lodge did not take part.[120]

There had been contact throughout 1837 between the Wigan brethren and another rebellious Masonic body named the Grand Lodge of Stockport, which, according to a letter sent to the Lodge of Sincerity in February of that year, was gaining some influence in the Manchester area. The leading lodge involved in this mysterious Grand Lodge was named St. John's Lodge, and in the letter they had claimed to have opened a lodge in Manchester called St. Alban's Lodge; and they were ambitiously about to open three more lodges. The Stockport Grand Master was called Ruben Hopwood, but there is no trace of him in the records of the UGLE. Gage was duly informed of the correspondence between the two Grand Lodges, though nothing seemed to have materialised in regards to the suggested union between them.[121]

Wigan's 'regular' lodge at this time – the Lodge of Antiquity, was going through a difficult period, and by 1841, they were in a very '*feeble condition*', having had very few new members over the previous years. Perhaps with this in mind, and the fact that the Wigan Grand Lodge had reinstated itself so strongly in the town, a communication had been received from the UGLE calling upon Masters of lodges to enforce the laws of the order, to promote the welfare of the Craft in general and in their own lodges in particular.[122] In contrast, the rebels were growing stronger, despite the overall downturn in Freemasonry in the north-west of England.[123]

---

[119] Read, *AQC*, Vol. 90, p.17.

[120] Ibid.

[121] Rogers, 'The Grand Lodge in Wigan', *AQC*, Vol. LXI, pp.193-5.

[122] Brown, *History of the Lodge of Antiquity No. 178*, p.38.

[123] See David Harrison, *Transformation of Freemasonry*, (Bury St. Edmunds: Arima Publishing, 2010). Chapter's 2 and 3 outline the difficulty that certain lodges in the industrial areas of the northwest

By mid 1842, Gage finally resigned from the Wigan Grand Lodge, angry at not being asked to review the re-numbering of lodges and the granting of new Warrants, a decision that had taken place in a meeting held on the 15th of August, 1838. The Wigan based Lodge of Sincerity became Lodge No. 1 (now being the leading lodge), and Gage's old Liverpool Lodge No.20, became Lodge No. 2, a move which may have added to Gage's anger and revealed how Wigan had become more dominant and more pro-active in the administration. However, this fresh pro-active stance by the new Wigan based Grand Lodge began to pay off; becoming more organised, meeting every quarter, and as a result, it spread its influence - having a total of six lodges under its jurisdiction by the early 1840s, though George Woodcock's Barnsley lodge had declined a fresh offer to join the revamped Wigan Grand Lodge, and the Kings Lynn lodge seemed to have thought twice about joining and had backed off.

The lodge based in nearby Ashton-in-Makerfield named Harmony and Perseverance became No. 3 after the Barnsley lodge had declined the invitation, the Lodge of Integrity – one of the original Wigan lodges to join the rebellion, became No. 4, another, named the Lodge of Knowledge in Warrington became No. 5,[124] and a new lodge - St. Paul's Lodge, which was based in Ashton-under-Lyne, to the east of Manchester, became No. 6 in October 1843.[125] St. Paul's Lodge was warranted after negotiations between the Wigan Grand Lodge and *'the Members of the St. John's and St. Paul's Societies'*, the discussions being mentioned in the minutes of a Grand Lodge meeting on the 14th of August, 1843, where, after hearing of the positive outcome of the *'Deputations that went to Ashton-under-Lyne'*, it was unanimously resolved that the brethren of these *'Societies'* were accepted under Wigan.[126]

There were later ambitious attempts at expansion; a lodge was warranted in 1846 in Blackburn called the Lodge of Truth, of which only scant information survives,[127] and there was discussion of forming yet another new lodge at Roby Mill near Wigan in 1847, but no further records have come to light regarding this mysterious lodge.[128] Another new lodge was mentioned later in the Grand

---

of England went through during the early nineteenth century, suffering low attendance, low membership and debt.

[124] Beesley, p.64-5.

[125] Ibid., pp.92-3.

[126] Ibid. Ashton-under-Lyne is not too far from Stockport; both being on the outskirts of Manchester, though there is no evidence to link the *'societies'* mentioned in 1843 with the Grand Lodge of Stockport, which had contacted Wigan in 1837.

[127] A rough draft for the Warrant for the new Lodge of Truth in Blackburn, dated 1846, was found as Fred Lomax and I searched in-between the blank pages of the main minute book of the Wigan Grand Lodge. A photograph of the draft Warrant is included here in the book for the first time. Beesley appears to have missed the document, but a mention of the Lodge of Truth at Blackburn appears in an undated Royal Arch Chapter record and is referred to in Rogers, 'The Grand Lodge in Wigan', *AQC*, Vol. LXI, p.200.

[128] Rogers, 'The Lodge of Sincerity, No. 1 of The Wigan Grand Lodge', *AQC*, Vol. LXII, p.46.

Lodge 'waste minute book' in a meeting on the 30th of June, 1856, being described as a '*New Lodge to be opened at the Rose Bridge Inn*'.[129] Not much else is known about this particular lodge; it was referred to as Lodge No.7 in the minutes of Sincerity and it may have ceased to operate a few years after, as there is no mention of it after 1858.[130] Despite its short life, it may actually be a contender for the most bizarre lodge in England; there is a strong tradition in Wigan that the lodge had held meetings on the canal tow path underneath Rose Bridge; with a Tyler placed at either end of the tow path to keep out intruders![131]

Gage had been given the title of Deputy Grand Master again in April 1838, courteously being given the task of overlooking some of the activities by correspondence. However, he was deeply upset that the 'Magna Charta' had been breached, as it had originally stated that on the creation of the rebel Grand Lodge, all lodge numbers per 1823 had been reverted back to their pre-union numbers before 1813. On the 10th of June 1842, Gage wrote a lengthy letter of resignation, in which he outlined his feelings at not being asked to review the decision of the new Warrants. He was a proud man, and as he was the person who had originally instigated the Liverpool Masonic Rebellion, he appeared to have been hurt by the decision. In the letter, he made references to the 'Magna Charta of Masonic Freedom', reminding the brethren of their origins:

'*It was therefore from an ardent desire to hand down to posterity the Ancient Landmarks Customs and Usage of Masonry that we re-established the Ancient Grand Lodge this act however could only justified by a strict Adhereance on our parts to the Ancient Laws Landmarks and Usages of Masonry.*'[132]

Gage also sternly refused a request to write a pamphlet detailing the causes of the rebellion. Despite Gage's coldness, he was still the spiritual leader of the 'Antients', and in the reply to his resignation, Gage was described by the Grand Secretary Robert Bolton as a man whom:

'*the tyrants in the Masonic world would have always looked upon with dread*'.[133]

Perhaps Gage's opinion was not sought by the Wigan Grand Lodge in fear of his reaction to the changes. The 'Magna Charta of Masonic Freedom', originally written under the influence of Gage, was re-written in 1839 as part of the reorganisation of the Wigan Grand Lodge.[134] This reorganisation, decided by a

---

[129] Rogers, 'The Grand Lodge in Wigan', *AQC*, Vol. LXI, pp.191-2.

[130] Rogers, 'The Lodge of Sincerity, No. 1 of The Wigan Grand Lodge', *AQC*, Vol. LXII, p.47.

[131] Arnold Singer, *The Grand Lodge of Wigan 1823-1913*, (Wigan, undated), p.5.

[132] An excerpt from Michael Alexander Gage's resignation letter, 10th of June, 1842, in Beesley, p.84.

[133] Ibid., pp.83-88.

[134] The 1839 version of the Magna Charta was hand-written in a leather bound note book and kept in a case with an inscription indicating it was presented to the Grand Master William Farrimond

Grand Lodge now dominated by Wigan brethren, began to forge a new cultural identity. The original rebels, Gage in particular, were still held in high regard, seen as the founding fathers of the resurrected 'Antient' Grand Lodge, and Robert Bolton's reply to Gage's resignation, though tinted with expectation and hinting at Gage's lack of interest, effectively left the door open for his return.

Gage however, never came back and never replied to Bolton's letter. Increasing the isolation of the Wigan Grand Lodge, Thomas Page and John Robert Goepel, two of the last remaining original rebels from Liverpool, returned to the United Grand Lodge on the 1st of December, 1858.[135] Like Gage, Goepel had dramatically changed his career, going from a jeweller to a dentist after the Masonic Rebellion, a profession that he engaged in until his death in 1862.[136]

Gage was by this time older and was still based in Liverpool, and though seemingly showing a lack of interest in Masonry, he still held a sense of importance when it came to his position within the Wigan Grand Lodge. His disinterest may have been as a result of disillusionment at his close colleague John Eden's embezzlement of Masonic funds, possibly the re-location of the Grand Lodge to Wigan, or perhaps down to Gage having a family and changing his career from a tailor to a Land Surveyor; Gage going on to publish his plan of Liverpool in 1835.[137] He was however, to remain a rebel to the end, effectively rebelling against the rebels. Gage was always an obstinate man, passionate, arrogant and confident in the face of opposition, and his fight for the cause of Antient Freemasonry had been extremely fierce and pro-active.

He held the respect of his fellow rebels, and without Gage, there would have been no Wigan Grand Lodge, his leadership influencing its original design. He had aspired to greater things; Gage, a mere tailor having written to the Duke of Sussex complaining about the way certain brethren in Liverpool were being mistreated, being an excellent example of an attempt to break down the class

---

Esq. This is now in the possession of Pemberton Masonic Hall. A photograph of the case is included here and a full transcription is presented in appendix I.

[135] Spurr, *AQC*, Vol. 85, p.42.

[136] Goepel's occupation is given as '*Dentist*' age 50, and his birthplace as London in the 1851 Census for Liverpool, Lancashire. Liverpool Library, Ref: HO 107/2180. However, Goepel was listed as a '*Jeweller*', aged 40 in the 1841 Census for Liverpool, Lancashire. Liverpool Library, Ref: HO 107/556/28. Deaths registered in June, 1862, John Robert Goepel, Liverpool. Ref: 8b. 113.

[137] Gage's occupation is listed as a '*Civil Engineer*' in the 1851 Census for Liverpool, Lancashire. Liverpool Library, Ref: HO153/2183, and in the Church Records for St. Peters, Liverpool; '*Baptism of William Henry, son of Michael Alexander Gage, Land Surveyor, & his wife Sarah*', 25th of December, 1833. Liverpool Library. Ref: 283PET2/21. Gage's occupation is also given as '*Land Surveyor*' in the 1841 Census for Liverpool, Lancashire. Liverpool Library, Ref: HO 107/558/3. A plan of Liverpool published in 1836 was based on Gage's expert survey of the port, see Liverpool Map, 1836, M. A. Gage, Maritime Archives and Library, Drawer Z/F3. A front page advertisements for the plan appeared in the Liverpool Mercury, 31st of July, 1835, issue 1256, p.1, and 16th of October, 1835, issue 1276, p.1.

and social divisions. Gage died in 1867 aged 79, though as Robert Bolton had noted, Gage would continue to inspire the Wigan Grand Lodge, and as we shall see, Gage's rebel days were far from over.[138] The success of the rebellion – albeit on a local basis - is revealed in its organization and the pro-active stance of the Wigan Grand Lodge, its effect on the United Grand Lodge proving permanent; with changes made to the Book of Constitutions and with the formation of the Eastern and Western Divisions of the large Lancashire province shortly after the revolt.

From its rebirth in 1838 and through the ensuing decade, the Grand Lodge of Wigan was at its height and revelled in its local status. Immediately after the decisive April meeting in 1838, on the 9th of May, the minutes of the Lodge of Sincerity referred to '*a Committee for managing the Business of the Re-formation of the Grand Lodge Bands & Aprons for Private Lodge when they where re-elected to manage the Whole Business untill the Coronation is over when a Play was proposed for the Use of the Grand Lodge*'; the Sincerity brethren were taking control of proceedings and celebrating their resurrection. This renaissance renewed their confidence after a period of healing and contemplation, though, as we shall see, this confidence was not to last, as the dream of the Wigan Grand Lodge disintegrated and unravelled.[139]

---

[138] Deaths registered in January, February and March, 1867, Michael Alexander Gage, aged 79, West Derby, Liverpool. Ref: 8b. 331.

[139] See Rogers, 'The Lodge of Sincerity, No. 1 of The Wigan Grand Lodge', *AQC*, Vol. LXII, p.44.

Copy of the
Circular of the Suspension of Francis
Duckinfield Astley Esq'. PGM for the
County of Lancashire.

_____

LS (Signed) Augustus Frederick GM

Kensington Palace
7th March 1822

Very Worshipful Brother,

In consequence of the irregularities which have taken
place in the management of the Interests of the Masonic
Fraternity of the Province of Lancashire, on which
subject an Investigation must take place I think it
most proper, That the Functions of the Provincial
Grand Master and his Deputy, should for that
period be placed in other hands; With this view I
request of you to take the immediate charge of the
Concerns of that Province, appointing a Brother
whom you may think duly qualified to assist in that
Investigation, as your Deputy, taking his Instructions
from you, until these important matters shall have
been explained, and the Grand Lodge shall have
come to a final decision therein.

For this purpose you will be so kind to adopt the
most prompt measures for informing the Provincial
Grand Master for Lancashire of my Pleasure on
this subject [...]

A copy of the circular of the suspension of Francis Dukinfield Astley by the Duke of Sussex, which is in the Rebel Committee minute book, dated the 7th of March, 1822.

MIGHTY ALEXANDER LONGSTITCH.

In the Press and speedily will be Published, a

NEW EDITION,

With bright, recondite, and erudite Annotations, Mystifications and Emendations of the last

"𝕻atljetic 𝕻oem,"

OF

PAUL PITILESS, Esq. POETASTER ;

Entitled "LONGSTITCH," by SIMON SAP, and his friend SNAP.

PRICE THREE PENCE.

The following is a short specimen of the Notes.

MIGHTY ALEXANDER,

The subject or *hero* of this poem, is no doubt some great *military character* whose actions are covered by allegory or fable. It has been thought by some, that *Alexander the great* is the high personage here introduced, and that "Longstitch" is a typographical error and ought to have been " *Longsword.*"—*Sap.*

It is astonishing to see the great folly of mankind on almost every subject in *common life*; and it was never more visible than in the conjectures of Mr. Sap, as to the " *hero*" of this poem. I should suppose, that the " *high personage*" is neither more or less than some poor Tailor, who forgot to "*cut his coat according to his cloth,*" and whose ▬ is attempted to be exhibited by Mr. P—— " Longstitch" might as well have been " Longneedle" or " Landmark" as "Longsword."—*Snap.*

P. M. OF THE SHOPBOARD.

By this P. M. it is clear the hero belonged to the army and was *paymaster,* and most probably belonged to the "*board of controul.*"—*Sap.*

It is a great pity that some people have no controul over themselves and their ideas, or my friend Sap would never have ventured to let so foolish an opinion have seen the light. P. M. I should suppose meant he was *past* being a *master :* i. e. he *had* once *been* a master tailor and was past it, and as he could not *ascend,* of course his motion must be retrograde.—*Snap.*

LIST! LIST! OH! LIST!

Nothing could be more clear that what I have before advanced as to the *profession* of the *hero* of this little poem. " List!" is a contraction or abbreviation for *enlist,* which means to *recruit,* and is applied to the act of engaging a young *soldier.*— *Sap.*

My friend Sap can hardly be such a *Johnny Row* (as a *soldier* would call him) to seriously imagine from the word "*list*" that the hero of this poem was a recruiting *sergeant,* when it is known to any child, that "list" is the selvege of woollen cloth, and is often used by little boys for garters. It is a word of contempt for a tailor, synonymous with " Snip !"—*Snap.*

FOR YOU MUST KNOW, &c.

It is well known that all soldiers are or ought to be *cutting youths*—the meaning is evident.— *Sap.*

The meaning is indeed evident—tailors being more in the *habit of cutting* than *soldiers.* I am informed by a friend of Mr. Pitiless, that this and the following line ought to run thus :—

" For you must know he is a *cutting blade*—
" Forsooth, a knight of the thimble, by trade !" *Snap.*

A KNIGHT, &c.

From this line there can be no doubt in the mind of the most prejudiced person as to the profession of the hero. We hear of Knights of the Garter! of the Collar! the Castle! &c. and why not of the *Thimble ?* For no doubt Alexander the Great might as well have instituted such an order as a certain notorious female did recently that of St. Caroline, (i. e. the " *Button-hole*") in Jerusalem.— *Sap.*

The hypothesis of my friend Sap is ingenious enough, but he ought first to have proved that *Thimbles* were in use in the time of Alesander the Great. It is as clear as the sun at noon day that " Longstitch" was a Tailor. A Knight of the Thimble being a well known designation or appellation of that industrious class of men (or fractional parts of men,) *Snap*—

Also in the Press and speedily will be Published, Sketches of the characters of the Button Street Star Chamber, in which will be introduced the Parentage, Education, life, and final exit of M. A. LONGSTITCH, Esq. Tailor in Ordinary to such of his Majesty's subjects as chuse to be neatly FITTED ; ▬▬▬▬▬▬ *of the Bishop, and other illustrious personages, by the Author of " Longstitch."*

'Mighty Alexander Longstitch', the satirical poem which cast Gage as a 'poor Tailor, who forgot to "cut his coat according to his cloth"'.

The original version of the 'Magna Charta of Masonic Freedom' signed by the Grand Master George Woodcock, Gage and other leading Masonic Rebels. Thanks to Martin Cherry, Library of the UGLE.

free and Accepted Masons of England,
according to the Old Constitutions, granted by
His Royal Highness Prince Edwin at
York. Anno Domini Nine Hundred Twenty and Six
as recorded in the Magna Charta of Masonic
Freedom.

COPY

In Deo nostrum fidem ponemus.

Whereas, the two great and In-
dependent fraternities, formerly known under the
denomination of Ancient and Modern Masons of
England, did associate themselves by a Treaty of Union
bearing Date the 1st Day of December 1813; from which
period this Grand Incorporated Body was to be known
and acknowledged by the Style and Title of the United
Grand Lodge of Ancient free and Accepted Masons
of England:

Therefore, be it known unto all
whom it may concern, that that part of the said
United Grand Lodge which is usually held in
London; have gradually Innovated upon the Ancient
Landmarks of Masonry in contravention of the Articles
of the aforesaid Union; and they have also composed

The first page of the main rebel Grand Lodge minute book showing the beginning of the 'Magna Charta of Masonic Freedom'.

My Son forget not my Law
but let thine heart keep my commandments
and remove not the Ancient Landmark which
thy Fathers have set.

Solomon

Signed

George Woodcock	G. M
M. A. Gage	D G. M
Ralph Ball	S G W
Thomas Page	J G W
John Eden	G Sect.y
J. G. Bennett P.M	492
Peter Brinbridge W.M	128
John Thompson P.M	128
Thomas Roberts S.W	20
Robert Hilton Sect.y	54
Robert Bolton P.M	492
Thomas Bullock W.M	54
James Cooper P.M	54
John Rutter	54
Laurence Marsden Sect.y	492
J. Sommerville (Scotland)	212
John Molyneux S W	54
Richard Sayer	492
W.m Green	54
Tho.s Strong (Ireland)	548
W.m Marshall	20

The rebels who signed the first 'Magna Charta of Masonic Freedom'.

Grand Lodge of Free & Accepted
Masons of England according to the Old
Constitutions holden at B: The: Johnson
Hole i'th Wall Market Place Wigan
April 13th 1838 A.L. 5842

The Grand Lodge was opened in Ample Form &
Solemn Prayer at ½ past Three O'Clock
When the following Brethren were Elected Grand
Officers for the year ensuing

William Farrimond Esqr. G.M.

M.A. Gage. D.G.M

B: Thos Page S.G.W B: Geo Daniels S.G.D
Jno Golding J.G.W. Warburton J.G.D
Edw Hedley G.T James Watts G.P
Robt Bolton G.S James Green G.T.

The Grand Secretary proposed that the Commer-
cial Hall be applied for immediatly on for the
Coronation carried
Proposed that the Masonic Committee make
Application for the said Hall
The Grand Lodge meet on the first Monday
In June
The Committee be requested to purchase 60
Yds Mazarine Blue Ribbon 3½ Inches Broad

That the Meeting of the Installation and
the Procession at the Coronation be inserted in the
Wigan Gazette previous to the meeting
When the Grand Lodge was closed in Ample Form & Prayer
The foregoing is a true copy of the minutes as above
dated   William Farrimond G.M

The re-launch of the rebel Grand Lodge; the minutes of the meeting at the Hole i'th Wall, Market Place, Wigan on the 13th of April, 1838.

The list of the Grand Lodge Officers elected before the procession through Wigan in honour of the coronation of Queen Victoria on the 28th of June, 1838. The signature of Grand Master William Farrimond can clearly be seen in the centre of the page.

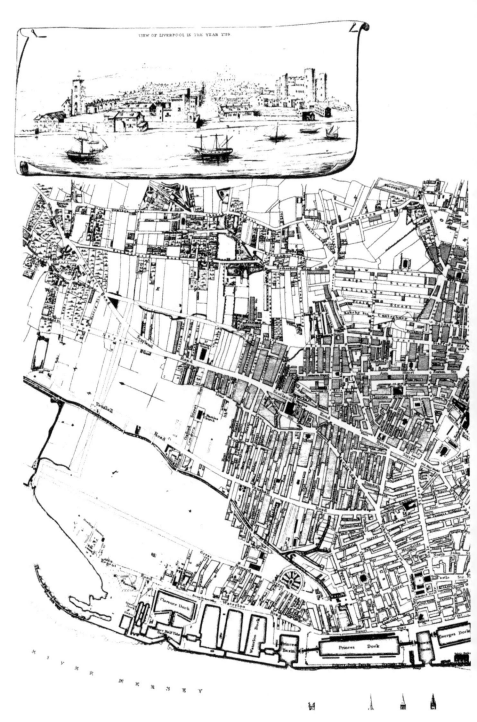

Precision and perfection sought: the plan of Liverpool by Michael Alexander Gage, 1836.

THE BLACK ROCK LIGHTHOUSE.

PLAN OF LIVERPOOL in the Year 1729.

LIVERPOOL

REDUCED BY PERMISSION FROM M.r PAGE'S
ELABORATE SURVEY.

Published under the Superintendence of the Society for the
Diffusion of Useful Knowledge.

SCALES

Dr Hughes Stone Quarries

Canning Dock
Salthouse Dock
Kings Dock
Queens Dock
Brunswick Dock

The hand painted Wigan Grand Lodge banner used in the procession on the 28th of June, 1838. (Photo by Fred Lomax).

Chapter 4
The end of the 'Antients'

'And furthermore be it known that they have therein introduced a Law for the purpose of enforcing obedience to what is styled by them, the established mode of working, this new system has been opposed and rejected by an imperative Masonic Duty, because it is not "according to the genuine Landmarks, Laws and Traditions of the Craft" as guaranteed by the third Article of the aforesaid Union...'

The Magna Charta of Masonic Freedom, stating the abhorrence for the new mode of working, 21st of July, 1823, Liverpool.[140]

'I only remember one tracing board, it was a piece of canvas about 4 ft square. On it were painted the three steps; pot of incense; Beehive; book of constitutions with tylers sword; All seeing eye; sword pointing to a naked heart; Anchor and Ark; Forty seventh problem of Euclid; Hour glass and scythe; The lamb; Jacobs ladder; Coffin with sprig of Acacia; and maybe a few more...'

James Miller, the last surviving member of the Lodge of Sincerity when it was under the Wigan Grand Lodge.[141]

'All I know about Wigan Grand Lodge is from the minutes for I was never a member. It had ceased to function before my time. But John Mort Snr. who was initiated in 1864, WM in 1866, 1869 and 1871 was appointed G. Master of Wigan Grand Lodge in 1886 and continued to the end.'

James Miller.[142]

Despite the revamping of the rebel Grand Lodge in 1838, its early success was not to last, and the Grand Lodge ran into difficulty; dogged by debt, arguments, internal disputes, expulsions and changing Grand Masters, it all started to fall apart, and the lodges under its sway one-by-one disappeared, their exact fate being somewhat of a mystery:

The Lodge of Knowledge No. 5 in Warrington, despite having got off to a promising start, seemed to have ceased working sometime around the later 1850s. Meeting originally in the King's Arms, they had taken part in a procession through the streets of Warrington on the 28th of June, 1841 to

---

[140] Beesley, p.25.

[141] *Reminiscences of an Unrecognised Lodge, namely Old Sincerity Lodge No. 486 by James Miller*, (1959), p.8.

[142] Ibid.,p.10.

celebrate the 'Antient' Masonic Festival of St. John,[143] and one of their members William Williams, had served actively as Junior Grand Warden in the Wigan Grand Lodge during the 1840s, rising to become the Grand Master in 1853, a position he served until 1855.

William Williams may be the same person who joined the Warrington based Lodge of Lights on the 28th of August, 1826, though he was not registered with the UGLE. Three years before, a member of the Lodge of Sincerity had joined the Lodge of Lights; James Asnip – a miller from Warrington who had originally joined Sincerity back in 1817.[144] The time of Asnip's joining – February 1823, could be a sign that he was seeking another lodge to join as the rebellion was reaching its height, although Asnip, like Williams, was also not registered with the UGLE.[145] Williams would have thus known about Sincerity and the development of the rebel Grand Lodge, and he certainly became a leading light in both the Lodge of Knowledge and the Grand Lodge. The Lodge of Knowledge had applied for its Warrant to the Wigan Grand Lodge in December 1838 '*When a Petition along with their Certificates of Seven Brethren praying for a Warrant to be held at Owen Cowley's King's Arms was read and agreed upon and ordered to stand No. 5.*'[146] So it appears that seven brethren (the number needed to form a lodge) – already Freemasons in Warrington, broke away and formed their own lodge, joining the Wigan Grand Lodge at the precise time it was reorganising itself. The Lodge of Lights was experiencing a period of decline at this time, and it is plausible that Williams could have assembled a number of brethren in a planned attempt to form a new rival lodge under a new Masonic body in an effort to revive Masonry in the town.

Despite Williams serving as Grand Master, they faded away and no trace of the lodge in Warrington has yet come to light. There is evidence of a possible member; the highly decorated Masonic grave of Charles Wainwright – who died in 1851 and is buried in St. Elphin's churchyard in Warrington, has elaborate symbols for the time showing the sun and the moon amongst other Masonic symbols (reminiscent of the symbols on the Wigan Grand Lodge banner).[147] It indicates on the grave that he was originally from Manchester, but as a Freemason, there appears to be no trace of him in the records of the Lodge of Lights or in the UGLE. Another member was a certain Brother Tomlinson who was briefly listed in the main minute book as seconding a motion during a

---

[143] See Rogers, 'The Lodge of Sincerity, No. 1 of The Wigan Grand Lodge', *AQC*, Vol. LXII, p.45 and in Beesley, p.80.

[144] See Rogers, 'The Lodge of Sincerity, No. 1 of The Wigan Grand Lodge', *AQC*, Vol. LXII, p.64.

[145] Membership lists of the Lodge of Lights, No. 148, Warrington, in the By-Laws book, (Warrington: John Walker & Co. Ltd., 1938), p.60.

[146] Beesley, p.65.

[147] See the picture of Charles Wainwright's grave. There is a Charles Wainwright who appears on the 1841 Census, living in Eccles; Salford Library, ref: HO107/543/13.

Grand Lodge meeting in 1840.[148] The Lodge of Knowledge met at a number of other locations in Warrington, namely Thomas Dennis' Union Coffee House in Dorman's Lane, and at William Thomason's Brittania Inn on the corner of Scotland Road and Butter Market Street, keeping a steady distance from the Lodge of Lights.

The Lodge of Integrity No. 4 ran fowl of the Grand Lodge of Wigan in July 1840 after getting into arrears. Charges were then laid against them by one of their own members – a certain Thomas Leigh, in the August meeting of 1842,[149] and they were summoned to appear at the next Grand Lodge gathering in October, of which only several brethren turned up, minus the Master and Wardens. Reconciliation was sought, but it was only in January 1844 that issues were finally resolved; a new Master was installed – a certain William Lancaster who had been Senior Warden in Lodge No. 1 took on the job *'in the time of their distress'*, and Lodge No. 4 was brought firmly back into the fold. The new Master then proposed a motion which said:

> *'that if any Brother or Brothers makes a proposition in any Lodge Under this Grand Lodge of Ancient Free and Accepted Masons of England to go under the United Grand Lodge of Free and Accepted Masons of England he or they so doing shall forfeit ten Shillings each and for the Second Offence shall forfeit Five Pounds each for the Lodge the offence is Committed and if he or they refuses to pay the fines so levied to be struck of the Lodge he or they belongs...'*[150]

This was a hefty fine for such an offence, and would have certainly made the brethren think twice of uttering such a blasphemy as a desire to return to the United Grand Lodge!

It seemed that a dispute may have taken place in Lodge No. 4 which resulted in some of the brethren considering going back to the UGLE. The fact that this old lodge – the 'Antient' Lodge of Integrity which had taken part in the rebellion at an early stage and on an equal setting with Sincerity, was numbered 4 in the new Wigan Grand Lodge listing, may have displeased the leading brethren of the lodge and led to a dispute with the Sincerity dominated Grand Lodge. Indeed, during a meeting in the Lodge of Sincerity on the 13th of April, 1840, it was noted that there were differences between the Wigan brethren and a committee had been appointed to settle them.[151] With appeasement in place, a number of

---

[148] Beesley, p.78. There was a William Tomlinson who joined the Lodge of Lights on 28th of September, 1812, though there is no mention of Brother Tomlinson's first name in the Wigan Grand Lodge minutes. See Membership lists of the Lodge of Lights, No. 148, Warrington, in the By-Laws book, (Warrington: John Walker & Co. Ltd., 1938).

[149] Beesley, p.89.

[150] Ibid., pp.95-6.

[151] Rogers, 'The Lodge of Sincerity, No. 1 of The Wigan Grand Lodge', *AQC*, Vol. LXII, p.44.

brethren from Lodge No. 4 were elected to serve as Grand Officers during the April 1844 meeting, and in March 1845, a brother of Lodge No. 4 – Geoffrey Hart, actually served as Grand Master '*Pro Tempore*' in the absence of William Farrimond Esq.[152]

Despite this new front of brotherly love, there were renewed hostilities in April 1846 when '*Brother Thomas Leigh, No.4 preferred a Charge Against Brother Jas. Hart for unmasonic conduct*'. Both had to wait until the September meeting for the outcome; '*When the Decision of the Grand Lodge in the case of Leigh versus Hart was that Leigh Asks Pardon for his conduct or to be suspended for twelve Months and Hart Asks Pardon for his conduct or to be suspended for six Months.*' Leigh subsequently asked for pardon, but Hart did not.[153] It was noted in the minutes of the Lodge of Sincerity on the 28th of May, 1855, that '*The furniture belonging to No. 4 Lodge to be brought to the room of No. 1*',[154] indicating that the lodge was still functioning at this point, and was working closely with Sincerity, and the very last mention of Lodge No. 4 was in 1879, when it was revealed in the 'Bye-law Book' that '*Members of Lodge No. 4 (are) to dine with No. 1 St. John's day, June 1879*'.[155]

The Liverpool Lodge No. 2 seemed to have finally disintegrated around 1858, the year when aging rebels John Robert Goepel and Thomas Page had finally returned to the UGLE.[156] Page had taken an active part as an Officer in the relocated Wigan Grand Lodge until the early 1840s, serving intermittently as Senior Grand Warden. As an original Liverpool rebel, Page was held in high regard by his Wigan brethren, his status being recognised when he served as Deputy Grand Master under William Farrimond during the procession through Wigan in honour of the coronation of Queen Victoria on the 28th of June, 1838.[157] However, as the Grand Lodge took on a wholly Wigan identity, the Liverpool lodge seemed to have become even more distant and isolated. One of Page's last mentions was in a list of the Grand Lodge Debts in December 1845; the old Liverpool rebel being owed £6, 5s.[158] Indeed, it appeared that the Wigan Grand Lodge had agreed to pay for Page's regalia, as a rather large Bill of £11, 15s. was mentioned as early as 1839.[159] As an original Liverpool rebel, Page was perhaps given special treatment in an effort to get him and his lodge to take part

[152] Beesley, pp.96-8.

[153] Rogers, 'The Grand Lodge in Wigan', *AQC*, Vol. LXI, p.188.

[154] Rogers, 'The Lodge of Sincerity, No. 1 of The Wigan Grand Lodge', *AQC*, Vol. LXII, p.47.

[155] Rogers, 'The Grand Lodge in Wigan', *AQC*, Vol. LXI, p.193.

[156] Thomas Page appears in the 1841 Census for Liverpool, aged 45, working as an engineer, and residing at Frederick Street, Upper Liverpool. Liverpool Library, Ref: HO 107/565/2.

[157] Beesley, p.81. Thomas Page was last appointed as Senior Grand Warden on the 12th of April, 1841, serving in the position for the '*ensuing year*'.

[158] Rogers, 'The Grand Lodge in Wigan', *AQC*, Vol. LXI, p.187.

[159] Beesley, p.69. Page's regalia Bill was by far the largest Bill listed in the Grand Lodge meeting on the 25th of March, 1839.

in the Grand Lodge. Goepel, unlike Page, did not take part in events in Wigan at all, and it seems that the Liverpool lodge simply dwindled away, with a few diehards lasting it out until the bitter end.

The Grand Lodge itself seemed to stagger to an administrative halt for a few years; the main minute book remaining blank for a number of years from March 1845, then suddenly restarting briefly in 1858, meeting half yearly, only to stop again in June 1860, with a final entry on the 18th of July 1866. The other lodges in Ashton-in-Makerfield and Ashton-under-Lyne also seemed to have stopped working by the 1860s; vanishing without trace, leaving Gage's original dream of a revival of the 'Antient's' in complete tatters.

The Decline of the Wigan Grand Lodge

To fill some of the gaps in the main minute book, we have to examine the Grand Lodge 'waste minute book' and the lost minutes of the Lodge of Sincerity; and it appears that the Wigan Grand Lodge soon started to get into trouble.[160] Financial problems had started to beleaguer the Grand Lodge by the mid 1840s; at a Quarterly Meeting of the Grand Lodge on the 28th of December, 1845, it was proposed by John Stephens from Lodge No. 4 *'That a Subscription for the Liquidation of the Grand Lodge Debt be raised by Annual Subscriptions to be paid ½ yearly by March and September and to be paid into the Grand Lodge at the said Meetings and the first half year to commence in March 1846.'* At the same meeting, it was also proposed *'That each Lodge appoint a Brother to be named a Commissioner for the liquidation of the Grand Lodge Debt and that they have the power to pay it as they think proper to the Liquidation of the said debt but to hold no Monies in their hands after the Meetings of March and September.'* On top of the new proposals, the Grand Secretary Robert Bolton volunteered to give up his salary of twenty shillings per year to the Liquidation of the Grand Lodge debt, and Bolton's action was followed by the Grand Tyler Thomas Green who also gave up his salary of twenty shillings to the same debt. It was also agreed to take on the same rate of interest as the Wigan Savings Bank instead of 5 per cent.[161]

In spite of these actions, the Grand Lodge continued to be troubled by debt, and during a meeting on the 15th of October, 1848, it was proposed *'that each Brother pay 6d. Annually for defraining the Expenses and liquidating the Grand Lodge Debt to commence March 1849.'*[162] The problems were compounded by the expulsion for fraud of the Grand Secretary Robert Bolton, which was mentioned in the meeting on the 26th of September 1847. Bolton was one of the origin rebels; he had joined the Lodge of Sincerity in 1813, and had been present at the first meeting of the rebel Grand Lodge in 1823, adding his signature to the Magna

---

[160] Both the waste minute book and the early minutes of Sincerity are currently missing, but they were both partly transcribed and discussed at length by Norman Rogers as the subject of his two papers for *AQC*.

[161] Rogers, 'The Grand Lodge in Wigan', *AQC*, Vol. LXI, pp.186-7.

[162] Ibid., pp.189-190.

Charta of Masonic Freedom. His expulsion must have sent shock waves through the Grand Lodge, and it can only be surmised at the feelings of betrayal and confusion that may have been felt by the Wigan brethren, perhaps reminding them of the other Grand Secretaries that had embezzled and mishandled funds in the mid 1820s.

There were also constant incidents of destructive drunkenness and abuse of the sick fund; on the 18th of May, 1840, the business of the Lodge of Sincerity had to be moved to the next lodge night *'in consequence of the intoxication of many of the Brethren'*,[163] and on the 19th of May, 1845, a brother was expelled for defrauding the lodge, assailing the brethren and damaging lodge furniture - he had come to the lodge *'in a beastly state of intoxication whilst on sick pay'*.[164] The previous year, a certain Brother Battersby had been expelled for receiving sick pay under false pretences,[165] and in 1864, Brother Matthew Holding was expelled for being drunk whilst working when he was receiving sick pay; he had fallen from his cart which was laden with timber in a drunken stupor.[166] Yet another member was expelled for drunkenness while receiving sick pay from the fund in 1884.[167] It seemed that not only the Grand Secretaries were apt to a bit of a fraudulent dabble.

Besides the financial problems, the Grand Master William Farrimond had not been turning up to the meetings; a number of Grand Lodge Officers had been standing in for him, such as the Senior Grand Warden Nathan Thomas in the meeting on the 4th of April, 1845, and Junior Grand Warden William Williams on the 22nd of September the same year. Isaac Kirk from Lodge No. 6 stood in for Farrimond on the 14th of September, 1846, and finally, in December, it was decided enough was enough, as James Wood of the Lodge of Sincerity was nominated and duly elected as Grand Master, replacing the much absented Farrimond. However, the election was declared void the following March *'in consequence of the representatives of St. Paul's Lodge'*, though James Wood was unanimously elected Grand Master again, and two members of St. Paul's Lodge No. 6 were elected as Grand Lodge Officers. St. Pauls' Lodge was still going strong at this point and was still meeting in Ashton-under-Lyne; Isaac Kirk taking a leading role as Deputy Grand Master during 1847. However, a year later, there were no members of St. Paul's Lodge within Grand Lodge, and from 1848 the lodge is hardly referred to.[168] Farrimond was never mentioned again in the minutes.

---

[163] Rogers, 'The Lodge of Sincerity, No. 1 of The Wigan Grand Lodge', *AQC*, Vol. LXII, p.45.

[164] Ibid., p.46.

[165] Ibid.

[166] Ibid., p.47.

[167] Ibid., p.49.

[168] Rogers, 'The Grand Lodge in Wigan', *AQC*, Vol. LXI, pp.188-9.

James Wood served as Grand Master until Warringtonian William Williams was elected to the position on Christmas Day, 1852. Wood had been fined 2/6 for non attendance on the 11th of July that year, and this may have affected his standing. Williams was installed the following year, but he only lasted a short time as Peter Seddon was installed as Grand Master on the 24th of June, 1855. This constant change of Grand Master reflected the start of a steady decline in the Grand Lodge, though under the long leadership of Seddon – who served until his death in 1886, the Grand Lodge would enter its final phase.[169]

The Memoirs of James Miller

James Miller originally wrote his memories of the Lodge of Sincerity in the late 1940s, stating that the Grand Lodge of Wigan survived, supervising the last remaining lodge; the Lodge of Sincerity, its last Grand Master being John Mort who served in the office from the 15th of February, 1886 until the lodge finally returned to the UGLE in 1913. Miller was a young man when he was initiated into the Lodge of Sincerity in 1908. He followed his father, his grandfather, and great-grandfather, in becoming a Freemason under the Wigan Grand Lodge, and he would become instrumental in the survival of its memory.[170]

Miller described many practices in his memoirs, some of which are now widely discontinued in English Freemasonry; such as the celebration of the festival of St. John, which had been celebrated by many lodges before the union. The ritual that he described was likened to parts of the York or Bristol working – two styles that have more of an independent and 'Antient' ceremony.[171] Miller also mentioned the practice of the Royal Arch as a fourth degree; its apron being worn by the Grand Master, John Mort, at all times. The Knights Templar and the Mark degree were also practised; with a travelling Mark Lodge occurring a number of times, such as in 1889 when ten brethren from Sincerity *'took a waggonette to Skelmersdale to put Bro. Roger Taylor through the Mark degree.'*[172] Miller also mentioned a sickness and burial society within the lodge, which was a continuation of the 'funeral fund' which was referred to in the minutes of the Wigan Grand Lodge in 1839. In all, what Miller described was a functioning local lodge that prided itself on its 'Antient' working and independent traditions.

---

[169] Ibid., pp.191-2.

[170] The memoirs of James Miller first appeared in Rogers' paper on the Lodge of Sincerity in *AQC* in 1951. A photocopy of the actual hand-written memoirs of James Miller was passed to me by Masonic historian Neville Barker-Cryer; these memoirs included more details about the events and workings of the lodge; such as the working tools and tracing board, and certain descriptions about re-joining the UGLE. This more comprehensive version was written by Miller in 1959, updating what he had previously written for Rogers over ten years before. Masonic historian Fred Lomax has recently transcribed the complete updated hand-written memoirs and they are kept at Pemberton Masonic Hall, Wigan, although they are presently not catalogued.

[171] Rogers, 'The Lodge of Sincerity, No. 1 of The Wigan Grand Lodge', *AQC*, Vol. LXII, p.76.

[172] Ibid.,p.50. There is a minute on the 20th of June, 1857 which mentions that Sincerity and Grand Lodge combined.

There is a note in the minutes of the 20th of June, 1857, that mentions that '*the Grand Lodge and the Lodge of Sincerity are now combining*', officially making Sincerity the leading lodge, although by this time, there wasn't that many lodges left under the Wigan Grand Lodge anyway.[173]

The sickness and burial fund appeared to be a central element to the Wigan Grand Lodge; for a brief period in the early 1840s a Doctor was appointed for the brethren, being paid 2/6 annually for each member. By November 1842, when the Doctor's services were terminated, the subscriptions were 1/- a month, with 1/- on the death of a member or his wife, and 6d. for any death in the Warrington Lodge. Funeral gifts were raised from £5 to £7 at this time.[174] This was an obvious attraction the Wigan Grand Lodge; the benefits of the fund being essential to a working man in an industrial town during the nineteenth century, the Grand Lodge competing with other local societies in the Wigan area, such as the Oddfellows or the Independent Order of Rechabites.

The sick pay and death benefit were mentioned numerous times in the minutes of the Lodge of Sincerity; both being raised at various points from the 1840s onwards in accordance to the condition of the lodge funds. Indeed, the Friendly Society aspects are clearly evident from reading the minutes of Sincerity; for example, on the 15th of July, 1878, it was declared that '*The Lodge lent Wigan Corporation £200 for 5 years at 4 per cent*', and on the 14th of February, 1881, it was mentioned that '*the interest from the £200 with the Corporation for this year be used for the purpose of a contingent fund to assist needy and distressed brothers.*' Five members were appointed to distribute the fund accordingly.[175] The lodge at this time was gaining profits from their money lending and could thus cover their needy brethren; their insured brethren were also securely covered, the management of the lodge certainly reflecting a benevolent society of the period. With the merging of Sincerity and the Grand Lodge in 1857, the Grand Lodge debts seemed to have been eventually eradicated, and the lodge was managing its finances more effectively.

John Mort seems to have held the Grand Lodge of Wigan together during its final years, and he appears in the main Wigan Grand Lodge minutes for the first time in 1866, when fellow Wiganer Peter Seddon was Grand Master.[176] Mort, like Miller, passed on his memories of the Wigan Grand Lodge, enabling Eustace Beesley to write his *history* in 1920. According to Miller, Mort was initiated in 1864; he served as Master of the Lodge of Sincerity on a number of occasions, and became the very last Grand Master in 1886. Since 1857 when the Grand Lodge had combined with Sincerity, the Grand Lodge was only ever mentioned after 1866 sporadically in the minute book of Sincerity; being opened

---

173 Rogers, 'The Grand Lodge in Wigan', *AQC*, Vol. LXI, p.192.

174 Rogers, 'The Lodge of Sincerity, No. 1 of The Wigan Grand Lodge', *AQC*, Vol. LXII, p.45

175 Ibid., p.49.

176 Beesley, p.103.

on special occasions, mainly coinciding with the Festival of St. John in December; such as on the 24th of December, 1881, when 'two members "past the Chair",[177] and on the 17th of December, 1902, when the Lodge of Sincerity was closed, then re-opened as 'the Grand Lodge of England under Prince Edwin of York', and '3 Brethren were made Past Masters'.[178] This occurred less and less, and Miller indicated that he was not a member (or an Officer) of the Wigan Grand Lodge, and that it had ceased to meet – Sincerity seemingly having integrated its function. He painted a cosy picture of an isolated lodge filled with a mixture of friends and family members; Mort's son, also called John, was a member, and Miller's uncle, Richard Warburton, was initiated on the same day as Miller was.

Miller joyously recited the merriment of the lodge festive board; where each member of the lodge was allowed one drink from the lodge funds. When the drinks had been consumed, the Worshipful Master would call out 'mortar', and a Steward would take the trowel around so each Brother could give his contribution to the next round of drinks. After these funds had been exhausted, a cry for 'more mortar' would ensure further drinks, accompanied by the fine tenor voice of John Mort Jnr., who was also a member of the Wigan Parish Church Choir. The installation ceremony of the Master was followed a few weeks later by the installation dinner, coinciding with 'The Festival of St. John', the occasion also being provided out of the lodge funds.

By 1908, the Lodge of Sincerity conducted its meetings in the Masonic Rooms at Leader's Buildings on King Street in the centre of Wigan, where incidentally, the local Orange Order met.[179] The building still survives and is adorned with Masonic symbolism, making it apparent that, although isolated, the Wigan Grand Lodge was at this time conducting its business under the noses of the local 'regular' lodges under the UGLE, such as the Lodge of Antiquity, which had actually met in the same building for a time before Sincerity moved there.[180] The Lodge of Sincerity was also obtaining its aprons, cases and ritual books from Kennings in London by this time; Kennings being the main supplier to the lodges under the UGLE, so the lodge was certainly moving in the same circles as 'regular' Freemasonry.[181] However, despite this tentative venture into open activity, they were still very much independent, and the lodge meeting room was set out differently to a 'regular' lodge – Sincerity using a large table (16 feet long) in the centre where the members sat. The chairs of the Master and

---

[177] Rogers, 'The Lodge of Sincerity, No. 1 of The Wigan Grand Lodge', *AQC*, Vol. LXII, p.49.

[178] Ibid., p.51.

[179] Ibid., p.52.

[180] See 'The Freemason', Vol. 40, (1902), p.549.

[181] Rogers, 'The Lodge of Sincerity, No. 1 of The Wigan Grand Lodge', *AQC*, Vol. LXII, p.52. The accounts of the Lodge of Sincerity on the 4th of July, 1910, show these orders from Kennings.

the Junior and Senior Wardens were situated around the table; the brethren seating themselves in-between these Officers.[182]

These eccentricities reflect the lodge as an apparent time capsule, having survived in isolation and having an 'Antient', independent and inward looking attitude. The drinking and socialising seemed to have created a deep bond between the brethren, keeping the last remaining lodge vibrant and alive. As we have seen, the Wigan Grand Lodge had previously met at numerous inns and taverns around Wigan, some meetings taking place in the centre of Wigan, such as the infamous Dog Inn at Wigan Market Place, where the Grand Lodge met on a number of occasions in 1839. Other meetings took place on the periphery of the Wigan area, such as the Angel Inn in Ashton-in-Makerfield. The use of these inns were vital as important meeting places for the Grand Lodge, many of them, like the Angel Inn and the Rope & Anchor Inn in Scholes, were run by fellow brethren, enabling the Grand Lodge to establish regular private meetings, ensuring its continuity and allowing it to carry on its own unique culture. However, there were occasional visitors from other lodges; such as on the 14th of September, 1867, when it was recorded that there were visitors from Ireland and Yorkshire.[183]

As the Wigan Grand Lodge descended into solitary isolation, with most of its lodges disintegrating, 'regular' Freemasonry under the UGLE flourished in Wigan; the Western Division of the Provincial Grand Lodge of Lancashire met there in October 1886, and in the November of the same year, the Wigan Freemasons under the United Grand Lodge celebrated the centenary of the Lodge of Antiquity No. 178. More visits by prominent figures within the United Grand Lodge followed; in October 1889, the Freemasons accompanied the Mayor to church and a sermon was given by the Grand Chaplain of England the Rev. T. Barton Spencer. Perhaps these very public displays by the ever more powerful and confident United Grand Lodge sent a message to the dwindling Wigan Grand Lodge.

Indeed, 'regular' Freemasonry in Wigan, like in other industrial towns at the time, attracted the local aristocracy. One such local aristocrat was James Ludovic Lindsay FRS, who resided at Haigh Hall, an elegant neo-classical manor house on the outskirts of Wigan.[184] Lindsay was to become the 26th Earl of Crawford and 9th Earl of Balcarres, and he founded the Lindsay Lodge No. 1335 in 1870, Lord Lindsay serving as Conservative MP for Wigan from 1874-1880.

---

[182] See the painting by James Miller of the layout of the Wigan Grand Lodge/Sincerity meetings at the Masonic Rooms at Leader's buildings, King Street.

[183] Rogers, 'The Lodge of Sincerity, No. 1 of The Wigan Grand Lodge', *AQC*, Vol. LXII, p.48.

[184] James Ludovic Lindsay was first initiated into the Isaac Newton University Lodge No. 859 in Cambridge in February 1866. He subsequently joined a number of other lodges including the Prince of Wales Lodge No. 259 in 1868 and the Lodge of Edinburgh No. 1 in 1870. Lord Lindsay – as he was styled from his grandfather's death in 1869 until he succeeded to his later titles on his father's death in 1880 – also served as Deputy Provincial Grand Master for West Lancashire.

Lindsay became as much a central figure for Freemasonry in Wigan as Sir Gilbert Greenall was in Warrington, and like Greenall, Lindsay became involved in the development of local education and charity; his family had been concerned in the opening of the local Mining and Mechanical School, and Lord Lindsay had been involved in the building of local school houses.[185] Lindsay became a celebrated astronomer, and, together with his father, they had built up one of the most impressive libraries in Britain; the *'Bibliotheca Lindesiana'*. In 1910, Haigh Hall played host to a visiting contingent of Manchester Masons, again confirming the power and status of 'regular' Freemasonry against the increasingly diminished and secluded Wigan Grand Lodge.[186]

Rejoining the United Grand Lodge of England

Miller was to witness the eventual end of the Grand Lodge of Wigan; its last surviving lodge being cut off and alone, and as a relic of the 'Antients' of the eighteenth century, it was not recognised by other local Masonic lodges. Actual Grand Lodge meetings had been sporadic since the 1860s, and despite the ruling passed in 1844 that it was forbidden to discuss joining the UGLE within the lodge meetings, it had been resolved in a meeting of Sincerity on the 12th of September, 1870, that they should join the *'London Grand Lodge'*, though nothing came of the decision and the idea was dropped.[187] Miller mentions that *'heated arguments'* on re-joining had been going on for two or three years leading up to 1913. This in itself was a sign of the end; the last rebel lodge had come full circle and it was time to go back into the fold.

The matter was brought to a head, as Miller puts it, in 1912, when an un-named newly raised brother received an invitation to visit a Masonic lodge under the United Grand Lodge of England. On presenting himself to the lodge, and showing his Wigan Grand Lodge certificate, he was refused admission, which led him to write a rather abusive letter, calling the lodge a bogus institution, and stating he was the victim of a fraud. This incident seemed to confirm that the Lodge of Sincerity, the last surviving lodge under the Wigan Grand Lodge, had a rather bleak future, and if it was to survive, it needed to adapt. Many 'regular' Masons were aware of the Lodge of Sincerity, and Miller stated that many used to ask for invitations to their ceremonies, but when told *'they could come if they invited us to their lodges'*, the discussion was ended.[188]

---

[185] See Cornelius McLeod Percy, *History of the Mining and Technical School, Wigan*, (Wigan, 1900). The Agent of the Earl of Crawford had chaired a Public meeting in 1857 which duly decided that the Wigan Mining and Mechanical School should be established. Many public buildings in the Wigan area bare the distinctive Crawford and Balcarres mark on the date stone, an example of one such building is the School House on Red Rock Lane near Haigh Village which was built in 1871.

[186] See Harrison, *Transformation of Freemasonry*, p.138-9.

[187] Rogers, 'The Lodge of Sincerity, No. 1 of The Wigan Grand Lodge', *AQC*, Vol. LXII, p.48.

[188] *Reminiscences of an Unrecognised Lodge, namely Old Sincerity Lodge No. 486 by James Miller*, (1959), p.20.

A meeting between both Grand Lodges was sought, and Sincerity was visited by Worshipful Brother J. D. Murrey from Provincial Grand Lodge, who was satisfied with what he saw of the working of the lodge. Miller recites that developments then moved quickly, and it was decided that the lodge could keep the name 'Sincerity' but would have to be renumbered. Ironically, the issue over the renumbering of lodges after the union was one of the reasons which had moved Gage to rebel against the United Grand Lodge in the first place. The lodge would lose its original number of 486, it would surrender its old Warrant, and despite being founded in 1786, it would have a new number of 3677. In the official United Grand Lodge records it would have the 26th of September 1913 as the date of its consecration.

All the brethren of the Wigan Grand Lodge then had to be initiated, passed and raised, in a ceremony which was reminiscent of the pre-union 're-making' ceremony; when an 'Antient' Mason joined a 'Modern' lodge. Miller seemed to have mixed feelings of his lodge rejoining the United Grand Lodge, and he ended his memoirs with a haunting image:

> '*But one can still wonder if the ghosts of those old brethren of an unrecognised Lodge still linger around Sincerity*'.[189]

Miller was speaking with some regret of the surrender of what was effectively the last surviving relic of the 'Antients' and was perhaps referring to the ghost of Michael Alexander Gage, still lingering in the lodge room with his Masonic rebels. It had been 90 years since Gage presided over the first official meeting at the Shakespeare Tavern in Liverpool, and in the Masonic Rooms, King Street in Wigan, Gage's dream finally ended - the last surviving lodge under the Grand Lodge of Wigan re-joined the United Grand Lodge of England, bringing the rebellion to an end.

---

[189] Ibid. Miller's regalia is currently held at the Library and Museum of the UGLE, such as his apron. Many thanks to the Rev. Neville Cryer who supplied a copy of the memoirs of James Miller.

Chapter 5
Life after the rebellion

'...a wicked conspiracy has been formed against Lodge 31, having for its object the extermination thereof'.

> The rebels of Lodge No. 31 writing in regards to their treatment by Deputy Provincial Grand Master Daniel Lynch, November, 1821.[190]

'...that the charge was the result of a deep-laid conspiracy in Liverpool in order to defeat the petition.'

> Gage talking in his defence to the House of Lords Select Committee, August, 1850.[191]

'for whilst the Lancashire Schismatics ultimately placed themselves altogether in the wrong, and beyond the pale of forgiveness, they took their stand – however, erroneously – on what they deemed to be a matter of principle...'

> R.F. Gould, *History of Freemasonry*, 1883.[192]

Those who remained loyal to the United Grand Lodge of England were greatly rewarded; Henry Lucas joined St. George's Lodge on the 26th of February, 1822, the lodge which was most antagonistic to Lodge No. 31. It became somewhat of a lodge of refuge for the brethren escaping Lodge No. 31 during this time, with a number joining throughout the rebellious period from 1819-1822.[193] Lucas was then duly appointed to be the first Provincial Grand Secretary for the newly created Western Division of the Lancashire Province in 1826.[194] James Spence, the Past Master of St. George's Lodge, who had led the opposition at the fateful Provincial Grand Lodge meeting in Preston in October 1820 to recall the 'memorial' to the Duke of Sussex, was designated as Provincial Junior Grand Warden on the 6th of March, 1822.[195] The Deputy Provincial Grand Master Daniel Lynch was reappointed to his office almost immediately after his

---

[190] See the transcribed collected letters and minutes of the Liverpool rebel Committee, from 26th of October, 1821 - 20th of May, 1822, pp.28-32. Liverpool Masonic Hall, Hope Street. Not listed.

[191] The Christian Times, 17th of August, 1850, Vol.11, No.111, p.4.

[192] R.F., Gould, *The History of Freemasonry*, Vol. III, (London: Thomas C. Jack, 1883), p.12.

[193] See *the membership list of the St. George's Lodge of Harmony No. 32, 1786-1836, C.D. Rom: 139 GRA/ANT/UNI, The Library and Museum of Freemasonry, UGLE, Great Queen Street, London.*

[194] See Rogers, 'The Grand Lodge in Wigan', *AQC*, Vol. LXI, p.198 and Spurr, *AQC*, Vol. 85, p.33.

[195] Rogers, 'The Grand Lodge in Wigan', *AQC*, Vol. LXI, p.198.

suspension, and aided William Meyrick who was placed in charge of the province after the suspension of the Provincial Grand Master - Francis Dukinfield Astley. Dukinfield Astley died aged 44, in July 1825, the experience of the rebellion having giving him *'great uneasiness'*. It was after his death, that the large and troublesome province of Lancashire was divided into the Eastern and Western Divisions.[196] Some of the rebels however, suffered a rather different fate, especially that of their spiritual leader.

Michael Alexander Gage took on the role of a dark Dickensian villain in the eyes of the United Grand Lodge, and certainly his life outside Freemasonry was full of intrigue and questionable deeds. He was an ambitious man who constantly strove to better himself and sought a higher status in life; writing pamphlets on engineering, designing a map of Liverpool and of course, designing a Masonic rebellion. His bankruptcy in 1821 was, as we have seen, a possible drive for his anger and frustration at the time of the rebellion, but he did manage to turn his life around soon afterwards; he changed his career from that of a tailor to a civil engineer, and by the late 1820s, he had busied himself with his magnum opus - the beautifully illustrated and intricate plan of Liverpool.

Gage had indicated his passion for the plan in a letter to George Woodcock in June 1828, outlining how *'he had been putting Masonry before business for too long and must devote himself to soliciting the inhabitants of Liverpool for subscriptions'*, he had even sent Woodcock a piece of the map. Gage went on to say that his *'projected plan of Liverpool which is now in the hands of the Engraver who has given me his Bond in the sum of £300 for its execution by 3rd (January 1829). I have therefore to furnish him from time to time with such parts of the Drawing as are immediately wanted.'* In the same letter Gage had declined to meet with Woodcock and his *'Barnsley friends'* at a suggested meeting in Manchester, and could not accept Woodcock's invitation to go to Barnsley at Christmas. Gage was leaving Freemasonry far behind and was embracing his new career as a civil engineer and cartographer with vigour.[197]

The map was advertised on various occasions in the Liverpool press, including the *Liverpool Mercury*, and also featured in various engineering journals from 1833 to 1839.[198] Many copies of the plan still exist today; some delicately hand coloured, fetching thousands of pounds on the antique market. It was publicised as being available in bound form, as well as mounted on linen in a case, or as a plain sheet, and, an edition of the map was also published by the celebrated London publisher John Weale,[199] who specialised in publishing low

---

[196] Ibid., pp.177-8. See also Spurr, *AQC*, Vol. 85, p.41.

[197] Read, *AQC*, Vol. 90, p.26.

[198] Liverpool Mercury, 29th of November, 1833, issue 1178, p.5.

[199] See the advertisement section in R. Armstrong, *An Essay on Boilers or Steam Engines: Their Calculation, Construction and Management, With A View To The Saving of Fuel*, (London: John Weale, 1839), p.272.

cost pamphlets and books on mechanical engineering and architecture. In advertisements for the plan, it was boasted that it held the patronage of none other than King William IV along with other assorted members of the aristocracy; including the Earl of Balcarres, Sir Robert Peel, and such eminent Liverpool Freemasons as William Ewart and General Isaac Gascoyne. The plan was dedicated to the Mayor of Liverpool and the common council.[200]

An advert for a '*corrected and completed*' plan, again stating its illustrious patrons, was placed on the front page of the *Liverpool Mercury* on the 16th of October, 1835, and it was accompanied by an additional advert in the form of a letter by Gage on another page, criticising Jonathan Bennison's map of Liverpool which was published in 1835. In the letter, Gage wrote of the '*very erroneous statement made in Gore's Liverpool Advertiser, of last week, relative to Mr Bennison's Map of Liverpool and its Environs.*' Gage was unmerciful in his attack on his fellow map maker, stating that the editor had inaccurately assured that '*every description of property is correctly delineated*', Gage asserting that '*with respect to a delineation of the distinct houses in Liverpool, the very reverse is the fact*', and that the advert for Bennison's map had '*a direct tendency to mislead the public, and having been copied verbatim into several other papers, I have considered it a duty which I owe to myself, as well as the public, to make this slight notice of the matter.*'[201] We can only surmise how thankful the public were for Gage doing this duty and saving them from being mislead in such a way.

Climbing the social ranks was still not easy during this period, not even for someone like Gage, who was educated and had a certain charisma, though he certainly had a talent for organisation, and sought perfection in his work; whether it was surveying a plan of the port of Liverpool or organising a Masonic rebellion. During the rebellion he had written eloquently to various lodges in England to gain support, and had surrounded himself with loyal supporters, so, writing to the most eminent men in the land in an effort to publicise his groundbreaking plan of Liverpool would be second nature. In 1841, he went on to write a pamphlet concerning the construction of a new dock and warehouses in Liverpool, having it published by the celebrated John Weale of London,[202] and Gage seemed to have the ear of the Liverpool Corporation in his advice on the construction of the new dock. His '*remarks*' to the Corporation pointed towards the combined dock and warehouse system - as seen in the construction of the now famous Albert Dock in Liverpool, which was opened in 1846.

---

[200] For the advertisement of Gage's plan of Liverpool showing its patrons see The Institution of Civil Engineers, *Transactions of the Institution of Civil Engineers*, Vol II, (London: John Weale, 1838), p.358. See also the Liverpool Mercury, 17th of July, 1835, issue 1263, p.8, and the Liverpool Mercury, 31st of July, 1835, issue 1265, p.1.

[201] Liverpool Mercury, 16th of October, 1835, issue 1276, p.1 and p.6.

[202] Michael Alexander Gage, *Remarks on the general construction of docks in the port of Liverpool, and strictures on the design of the intended new dock and warehouses: Addressed to the corporation and the rate payers ...*, (London: John Weale, 1841).

Gage's eloquent writing skills and the fact that he had successfully published his plan of Liverpool and his pamphlet, may have been a reason behind the request made by the Wigan Grand Lodge in 1842 for Gage to prepare a pamphlet on the cause of their '*Secession*'. Gage briskly declined saying he could not '*perceive any good end that would be attendant upon the publication of such a document...*'[203] Being the leader of the rebellion, he would have been best placed to comment on the events, but his newly found publishing contacts would have assisted in getting the pamphlet published and distributed, perhaps even spreading the word of the newly organised Wigan Grand Lodge.

Slowly, Gage was gaining an elevated social position in Liverpool - a town which thought of itself as the major port in Great Britain and a rival to London. His plan of Liverpool adorned the libraries and studies of some of the most eminent men in the country, his advice was sought by the Liverpool Corporation, he had achieved publication by none other than John Weale - a man who had many friends in the scientific community of the period, and he was entering local politics. It was however to all go wrong for Gage; his life not being dissimilar to the intricate plot of a Dickens novel, ill judgement, eagerness to climb the social ladder and his obstinate and vindictive character hastening his downfall.

Gage and the Liverpool Corporation Waterworks Bill

Liverpool in 1846 was '*one of the unhealthiest towns in the country; and one of the chief causes of this was alleged to be the impurity and deficiency of the water supplied to the town*'.[204] The Liverpool Corporation Waterworks Bill was a means in which fresh water from a series of reservoirs near Rivington Pike – a hilly area close to Wigan - could be piped 27 miles into Liverpool. The Bill's supporters were thus named '*Pike-ists*', but a group of Liverpool residents were fiercely against the scheme and were determined to fight it all the way. At the time, water was in short supply to the growing port, and only available to those who could pay for it; business interests coming before the interests of public health as two private water companies supplied the town with water – mainly taken from local wells, which were very often polluted. Cholera and other diseases had recently ravaged the rapidly expanding town of Liverpool, and clean water was much needed.

As the railways had gained its supporters and critics, the new waterworks schemes also had their critics, and Liverpool's scheme was to be the largest and most ambitious project to date. Gage became a stern critic of the scheme; he was an old fashioned man and by this time he was in his late 50s, but the scheme was to fuel his anger for more personal reasons, and would give the old rebel one last cause to fight against.

---

[203] Beesley, pp.83-4.

[204] Liverpool Mercury, 4th of April, 1848, issue 1975, p.5.

Gage, now being a renowned local surveyor, had undertaken work on behalf of the Corporation of Liverpool with his son, from September to November 1846, and had come to the conclusion that an alternative water source could be used other than the Rivington Pike scheme, Gage stating that '*an inexhaustible supply of excellent water may be procured within a range of two miles from the centre of the town, by means of Artesian Wells and borings.*' Gage however, believed that the Corporation had already adopted Rivington Pike as its '*pet scheme*' and when he felt that the Corporation had not paid him enough for his survey, in an un-presidential move, he took the Mayor and the Corporation to court for unpaid wages. To exemplify Gage's professional standing, his plan of Liverpool was shown in the court as '*a work of skill almost unparalleled in the history of the country*', and it was suggested that Gage's report should be examined '*instead of favouring projects which were at once chimerical and wild*'. A verdict was taken for Gage and an agreement on the matter of unpaid money reached.[205]

Gage had been right about the Council's plan; the Town Council had bought out the two private water companies which had supplied Liverpool with water and the Liverpool Corporation Waterworks Act was passed in 1847. The Council had commissioned the leading water engineer Thomas Hawkesley to construct the reservoir at Rivington Pike and bring the precious clean water into Liverpool. Gage's proposals of using local wells had been passed over in favour of Hawkesley's Rivington Pike scheme, leaving Gage incensed that his professional standing was under question and his pride hurt.

With his anger ignited, in March 1849, Gage published a long letter in the *Liverpool Mail* sternly putting forward how he had a viable alternative to the Rivington Pike scheme '*proving the abundant resources at command for a home supply of water*'. Gage concluded that a number of the wells, which, despite Thomas Hawkesley's assertion of them as being effected by '*over pumping*', were still very much '*inexhaustible*' with an abundant supply of water. Gage was taking on Hawkesley and the Corporation directly in his usual aggressive manner; the letter including his own figures and measurements taken from the wells to discredit and disprove Hawkesley's own conclusions. He attacked Hawkesley for having a lack of local knowledge regarding the geology, and called his statement of the wells being affected by too much salt as '*absurd*'. Gage concluded his letter by commenting on '*the delusive and disastrous Rivington Pike scheme*', stating with disgust '*the highly reprehensible conduct of those parties who have been instrumental in forcing it upon the rate payers.*'[206]

It was as if Gage the rebel had embraced another cause; his rage and his passion against the Rivington Pike scheme was boiling over into an aggressive war of words in the courts and the press. In May 1849, Gage attended a dinner

---

[205] Ibid.

[206] Gage's letter to the Liverpool Mail was also published in the Liverpool Mercury, 20th of March, 1849, issue 2075, p.4.

and presentation to Mr. Councillor Henry Gordon Harbord at the Great George Tavern in Upper Pitt Street; it was an anti-Pike-ist gathering of various local dignitaries and supporters, where it was stated that '...*the Pike scheme, and the frightful act of Parliament, which would literally have ruined the town, were doomed, and would soon be consigned to the tomb of the Capulets*'. Gage's work against the scheme was duly noted, and he was toasted as a man '*who had afforded so much valuable information to the public on the question of the home supply of water*', a declaration which was followed by loud cheers from the gentlemen present. Gage returned thanks in a somewhat typical scientific speech, relishing in his new found adoration as a rebel with a new cause.[207]   The dinner certainly resembled a time when, as Deputy Grand Master of the rebel Grand Lodge all those years before, Gage would have took great pleasure in the importance and value of his position during the festive board of a Grand Lodge meeting.

Gage had been unanimously re-elected in the February as a representative to the Council of the Confederation at a general meeting of the members of Abercromby Ward, Gage by now being deeply active in local politics; the thanks of this particular meeting being given to the chairman of the Dock Committee for '*his firm determination to maintain the rights of the Corporation as trustees of the Liverpool Dock estate, and for his great exertions in thus protecting the interests of the rate-payers.*' Harbord had also been active in February; attending a meeting of the Toxteth Park Branch of the Constitutional Association to organize a defence of the navigational laws.   At the meeting, it was stated that '*any change in the fundamental principles of the navigational laws would injure the shipping interests of the country*', and '*that their abrogation would be fatal to the commercial prosperity of this country*'. A resolution was moved to petition the House of Lords to reject the Bill, the essence of the meeting being somewhat similar to the stance on the Waterworks Bill; certain like-minded Liverpool political activists engaging to protect their interests.[208]   Indeed, there was a culture of petitioning in Liverpool which dated from the later eighteenth century; petitioning being a traditional method of putting forward concerns and grievances, and of course, to seek reformed legislation.   Liverpool's merchant and business community had found a voice very early on with its Chamber of Commerce, and had relentlessly targeted Westminster on numerous occasions from 1774, through lobbying, petitioning and representation.[209]

Events came to a head when a new Bill aiming to amend the Liverpool Corporation Waterworks Act was presented to the House of Lords on the 6th of

---

[207] Liverpool Mercury, 11th of May, 1849, issue 2090, p.8.

[208] Liverpool Mercury, 20th of February, 1849, issue 2067, p.4.

[209] Robert J. Bennett, *The Voice of Liverpool Business: The First Chamber of Commerce and the Atlantic Economy 1774-c.1796*, (Liverpool: Liverpool Chamber of Commerce, 2010), p.8 and p.120. Bennett's excellent work examines how the Liverpool Chamber of Commerce – made up of Liverpool bankers, merchants, ship owners, slave traders and assorted local business men (and women) created a voice to effectively protect their interests.

June, 1850; proposing an extension to the time limited by the original Act, for purchasing land and constructing the works.[210] In response, a petition was hastily conducted against the Bill, with Gage being directly involved; promoting and organising the petition. The petition revealed thousands of signatures when presented to the House of Lords on the 17th of June, 1850,[211] seemingly showing that a large amount of Liverpool rate-payers were firmly against the Rivington Pike scheme. However, they were suspiciously all collected in a relatively short space of time showing page after page of the same handwriting, arousing the suspicion of the Lords immediately.

An inquiry was conducted by a Select Committee in the House of Lords and a number of '*agents*' who had gathered the signatures were questioned throughout July, the result of which was that, as the main promoters of the petition in opposition to the Bill, Gage and Liverpool solicitor Charles Gream of Temple Street, were found '*consequently responsible for its Integrity and have been guilty of gross Neglect, not having taken the necessary precautions to prevent Fraud*'.[212] Gage and Gream were subsequently called to the bar of the House of Lords on the 13th of August, and on the motion of Lord Monteagle, were charged with fraudulently adding thousands of fake signatures to the petition. Gream, in his defence, declared that there had been a '*very short time in which to get up the petition, and that the fictitious signatures were not discovered until within thirty-six hours of the time at which it was necessary to present it.*' In typical Gage fashion, and with arrogance and self righteousness not unlike that seen in his rebellious letters and documents all those years ago, he declared '*that the charge was the result of a deep-laid conspiracy in Liverpool in order to defeat the petition.*'[213] Both men were duly found guilty and were sentenced to serve a fortnight at Newgate prison in London.[214]

After their brief but harrowing time in Newgate, Charles Gream subsequently emigrated to Canada with his wife, and settled in Ontario, setting himself up as an attorney and starting a new life.[215] Gage returned to Liverpool, but, just like a hapless character from a Dickens novel, he soon found himself in trouble once

---

[210] *Journals of the House of Lords*, Volume 82, (London: Parliament, House of Lords, 1850), p.190. On the 6th of June, 1850, '*a Bill intituled to extend the time limited by the Liverpool Corporation Waterworks Act 1847, for purchasing lands and constructing the works, authorized by such an Act, and for other purposes, (herein-after designated as the "Liverpool Corporation Waterworks Bill")*'.

[211] *Journals of the House of Lords*, Volume 82, p.262.

[212] Ibid., p.419.

[213] The Christian Times, 17th of August, 1850, Vol.11, No.111, p.4.

[214] *Journals of the House of Lords*, Volume 82, p.478.

[215] Canadian 1881 census, Ontario; Charles Gremes, Attorney aged 71 and his wife Sarah, both born in England. Film history library film 1375874, NA film no. C-13238, District 122, sub district D, page no. 9. See also 1851 census for Liverpool; Charles Gream, Solicitor aged 41 and his wife Sarah, Ref: 575A, 2188/4, Liverpool Library.

more; his debts had mounted, and he found himself appearing before the Court for Relief of Insolvent Debtors on Friday 10th of October, 1851.[216]

Until 1841, the legal status of being a bankrupt was confined to traders owing more than £100, though this was reduced to a sum of £50 in 1842. Gage had been a trader when, in 1821, he had become bankrupt, but at this time, debtors who were not traders did not qualify to become bankrupt, so Gage stayed as an insolvent debtor. Responsible for his debts but unable to pay them, Gage remained subject to common law proceedings and could languish in prison indefinitely if his creditors so desired. Insolvent debtors were held in local prisons and attended County Courts, and Gage was remanded in Lancaster Gaol for two months,[217] as Liverpool was then in Lancashire. Imprisonment for debt did not cease until 1869, but there was however, the Court for the Relief of Insolvent Debtors, which had been established in 1813 - an insolvent debtor, like Gage, could apply to a Justice of Peace and submit a schedule of their assets.[218]

Gage's appointed Asignee was Peter Laurie Mactaggart, a tailor from Liverpool – the same trade Gage had plied all those years ago; it appears that Gage *'for got to "cut his coat according to his cloth"*.[219] Gage finally got released, and, in 1852, he made a comeback as a surveyor, advertising his *Statistical Diagram; exhibiting, by fluxional curves and lines, a view of the progressive increase of population, tonnage and dock duties in the port of Liverpool from 1700-1851; also, the comparative increase of tonnage in the port of London.*[220] This was a typical scientific diagram of the period which could be used as a decorative reference chart; it had the special patronage of his Royal Highness Prince Albert - showing that Gage had not lost his touch in advertising his skills of master-craftsmanship, but it also put forward the vital importance of Liverpool to the economy of Great Britain and its rivalry with London.[221] Gage's fellow anti-Pikist associate Councillor Henry Gordon Harbord had died in December 1849,[222] and the Liverpool Corporation

---

216 See *The Jurist*, Volume 15, Part 2, for the year 1851, (London: V. & R. Stevens & G. S. Norton, 1852), p.387. Michael Alexander Gage, Civil Engineer of Liverpool was appointed the Assignee Peter Laurie Mactaggart, case no. 74,251. See also *The London Gazette*, 24th October, 1851, Issue No. 21256, p.2808, Court for relief of Insolvent Debtors.

217 Liverpool Mercury, 21st of October, 1851, issue 2338, p.8.

218 See the National Archives website: http://www.nationalarchives.gov.uk/records/research-guides/bankrupts-insolvent-1710-1869.htm [accessed on the 24th December, 2011]

219 The London Gazette, 25th of September, 1883, issue 25272, p.4692, which states the occupation of Peter Laurie Mactaggart of Liverpool as a *'Tailor, Draper...'*

220 Michael Alexander Gage, *A Statistical diagram exhibiting by fluxional curves and lines a view of the progressive increase of population, tonnage and dock duties in the Port of Liverpool from ... 1700 to 1851: Also the comparative increase of tonnage in the Port of London during the same period, etc*, (London: Saunders and Stanford, 1852).

221 Liverpool Mercury, 6th of May, 1853, issue 2499, p.3.

222 Liverpool Mercury, 4th of January, 1850, issue 2156, p.2.

Waterworks Amendment Act was dutifully passed in 1850, the scheme being finally completed in 1857.[223]

Gage died in 1867 aged 79, though his eldest son, Michael Alexander Gage Jnr.,[224] continued his father's work as a civil engineer after an early career as an analytical chemist, moving to Rhuddlan in north Wales, where he died in 1901, also aged 79.[225] Gage's ultimate undoing had been his vindictive and aggressive character; he was a rebel until the end.

John Robert Goepel became a dentist, and finally returned to the UGLE, being reinstated on the 1st of December, 1858. He died in 1862, but his son, also called John Robert Goepel, continued to work as a renowned Liverpool dentist, and also became an extremely renowned Liverpool Freemason.

John Robert Goepel Jnr. became heavily involved in a number of Liverpool lodges; he was initiated into the Harmonic Lodge in 1856, though he had resigned from the lodge by 1859. The brethren of the lodge must have been aware of his father's rebel past, and his entrance into Liverpool Masonry at this time may have aided his father's return into the fold. Goepel Jnr. then went on to join the illustrious Everton Lodge No. 823, serving as Worshipful Master in 1863,[226] and had also joined the Lodge of Perseverance No. 155 in 1864, becoming Worshipful Master there in 1866.[227] In 1868, along with a number of other local Freemasons attached to the Everton Lodge, they petitioned for a new Chapter called the Everton Chapter to meet at the Masonic Hall at Hope Street, Liverpool.[228] Goepel was also a member of a Chapter which was attached to his old Harmonic Lodge, and is recorded as being 1st Principal in 1877.[229] He was even present at the laying of the cornerstone of the new

---

[223] The London Gazette, 22nd of November, 1889, issue 25986, p.5803. A listing of the Liverpool Corporation Waterworks Acts is presented, including the original Act of 1847 and the Amendment Act of 1850.

[224] The London Gazette, 18th of November, 1859, issue 22327, p.4173. Here, Michael Alexander Gage's son, referred to as 'the younger' or 'jr.' had his partnership dissolved in the business of 'Manufacturing Chemists' but he continued in this line of work until later in his life, and appears in the 1881 Census returns as a civil and mining engineer. See 1881 Census, Brynyscawen, Rhuddlan, Ref: 5527/106, p.2. Denbighshire Archives.

[225] Deaths registered in September, 1901, Michael Alexander Gage, aged 79, St. Asaph, Denbighshire. Ref: 11b. 196.

[226] See *A History of the "Everton Lodge" No. 823, Liverpool, 1860-1910*, (Liverpool, 1911). See also 'The Freemason', 28th of August, 1869, p.100.

[227] See the membership list for the Lodge of Perseverance No. 155, Liverpool, 1864. Library and Museum of UGLE. See also Anon. *A Brief History of the Lodge of Perseverance No.155*, (Produced by the lodge and undated), p.9.

[228] See 'Freemason's Magazine and Masonic Mirror', Vol. XIX, (New Series) July to December 1868, (London: Freemason's Magazine Company, 1868), p.397.

[229] See Rogers, 'The Grand Lodge in Wigan', in *AQC*, Vol. LXI, p.198.

Masonic Hall at Hope Street on the 2nd of November, 1872, Goepel Jnr donating the coins that were set under the stone in the ceremony.[230]

Everton Lodge was one of a small collection of eclectic lodges in Liverpool that had emerged during the mid-late nineteenth century that practised a unique version of ritual working loosely termed the 'Bottomley' ritual - a style specific to Liverpool, and one that retained various 'Antient' elements. One of the results of the rebellion was that the UGLE took a reviewed stand on lodge ritual working; '...*that the members present at any lodge have an undoubted right to regulate their own proceedings, provided they are consistent with the general laws and regulations of the Craft.*'[231] The working of the 'Bottomley' ritual reflects this stance; the ritual differing slightly in each lodge that practises it; the ceremony being peculiar to each particular lodge. It seems to celebrate the joy of independent ritual working; however, it stays close enough to emulation ritual practiced by the UGLE, but is far more descriptive in places, using additional explanations to embellish the ritual, which ultimately produces more flourish and a certain Victorian fancy in parts. The ritual performed in the Toxteth Lodge No. 1356 for example refers candidly to '*Ancient Freemasonry*', especially in the first degree and each lodge that practices 'Bottomley' fiercely defend their individual working.[232]

Lodges which practiced the 'Bottomley' working had begun to appear in the port by the mid nineteenth century, such as the Downshire Lodge No. 594 which was constituted in 1851 and was a daughter lodge of the Merchants Lodge. Everton Lodge was consecrated in 1860, and it was brethren from these lodges that founded the Toxteth Lodge in 1871, which also became a 'Bottomley' lodge. These were followed by other lodges, such as Yachtsman's Lodge No. 3698, which was warranted in 1913, and St. Peter's Lodge No. 4324, consecrated in 1921, which became one of the last 'Bottomley' lodges to be founded. The older lodges of Liverpool, such as the Merchants Lodge, which had members that had been actively involved in the rebellion, also practices an independent version of the ritual; the working differing in parts to the way other lodges conduct their ceremony. Another lodge involved in the rebellion – the Mariners Lodge, of which Goepel Snr. was originally a member, also has its own version of the ritual, both these lodges having done so from at least the nineteenth century.

---

[230] See *A Brief History of the Lodge of Perseverance No.155*, p.9.

[231] See Rule 181 referring to Private Lodges in *The Constitutions of the Antient Fraternity of Free & Accepted Masons under the United Grand Lodge of England,* (London: UGLE, 1919), p.92. Also see Spurr, *AQC*, Vol. 85, p.43.

[232] The differences can be examined when looking at all the various lodge ritual books, most of which are privately published by the particular lodge. Some lodges who work 'Bottomley' have had hand-written versions of the ritual passed down through the years for the purpose of memorising it for the ceremony, so over the years, differences occur in the particular lodge working.

If there was an important Masonic function in Victorian Liverpool, Goepel Jnr. was almost certainly going to be present. One such function saw him serve as a Steward at the Grand Masonic Ball which was held at Liverpool Town Hall in January 1864 in aid of the funds of the West Lancashire Masonic Educational Institution; Goepel assisting in receiving the prestigious guests which included the likes of Lord and Lady Skelmersdale, Lieutenant-Colonel Sir Thomas George Hesketh, Bart., M.P., Lady Arabella Hesketh and the Mayor of Liverpool. The Ball was stylishly reported in the Liverpool Mercury, giving a complete description of the elegant event which would have certainly made Michael Alexander Gage grimace with displeasure:

> '*In front of the orchestra of the large ballroom was suspended the magnificent banner of the Grand Lodge, on which are emblazoned the Freemasons' Arms, quartered with those of the county of Lancaster, and the arms of the Provincial Grand Lodge. The supper room was appropriately decorated with the numerous and richly-emblazoned banners of the Chapter.*'

A vast glittering array of Masonic regalia was worn by a variety of Orders during the Ball: '*some of the Knights Templar appeared in the long, flowing white mantle of their order, with the cross of the crusaders upon the shoulder*' and '*Several gentlemen wore military and naval uniforms as well as elaborate Masonic adornments.*'[233]

Goepel Jnr. was also involved in the Knights Templar, being a member of the Liverpool Conclave No. 55; appearing at the "Red Cross" Conclave, in October, 1871,[234] and at the Conclave of the Knights of Rome and the Red Cross of Constantine at the Adelphi Hotel, which was opened by none other than '*Sir Knight J. R. Goepel M.P.S.*'.[235] It seems there was hardly a Masonic social event, Provincial Masonic meeting or Masonic funeral[236] that Goepel Jnr. did not attend. At a reported '*Great Gathering of Freemasons*' held at Liverpool Masonic Hall in 1876, Goepel Jnr. was part of a committee that dealt with the charity funds, and Goepel put forward that '*a sum of not less than 100 guineas be paid from the charity fund to the Royal Masonic Institution for Girls*', the educational and charitable ethos of Masonry obviously appealing to him.[237] His Masonic activity was reaching exceedingly dizzy heights, and it was no surprise that Goepel was to be present at one of the largest Provincial Grand Lodge gatherings to have '*hitherto been witnessed in connection with the province of West Lancashire*' in Chorley, near Wigan, in October 1880, with Deputy Grand Master and Provincial Grand

---

[233] Liverpool Mercury, 13th of January, 1864, issue 4970, p.6.

[234] Liverpool Mercury, 27th of October, 1871, issue 7414, p.6.

[235] Liverpool Mercury, 19th of July, 1873, issue 7955, p.7.

[236] Liverpool Mercury, 9th of January, 1878, issue 9356, p.6, a Masonic funeral in Liverpool was reported, with '*upwards of 150 brethren present*', including J. R. Goepel, P.P.G.D.C.

[237] Liverpool Mercury, 5th of October, 1876, issue 8961, p.7, the '*Great Gathering of Freemasons*' was a Provincial Grand Lodge meeting.

Master of West Lancashire the Earl of Lathom directing an estimated 500 Masons in the meeting.[238]

It was at a Provincial Grand Chapter of the Royal Arch however that Goepel Jnr. was to become close to his father's rebel spirit and the Wigan Grand Lodge, when, with Lord Skelmersdale presiding, they met at the newly opened Masonic Rooms in Leader's Buildings, King Street, Wigan, in April 1874; the very rooms where the Wigan Grand Lodge came to an end in 1913. Lord Skelmersdale was so pleased with the *'elegant building'* that *'His hope was that such an excellent example as had been set in Wigan might be followed throughout this great province, and that they might be truly able to say no province could excel West Lancashire'*.[239] His speech, which along with the event, was reported in the Liverpool Mercury, could almost have been directed at the dwindling Wigan Grand Lodge.

Goepel Jnr. became a highly esteemed dentist residing on the corner of Mount Pleasant and Rodney Street - an extremely respectable area on the outskirts of the port,[240] and he featured in numerous dentistry registers and journals, such as 'The Transactions of the Odontological Society of Great Britain' in 1879.[241] Despite his activity at such a high Masonic level, he certainly continued his father's passion for the right to work traditional and independent Masonic practices in Liverpool, best exemplified by the working of the 'Bottomley' ritual – a ritual style unique to the port.

James Miller remained a member of the Lodge of Sincerity after the lodge had rejoined the UGLE in 1913, becoming Worshipful Master in 1921 and Treasurer in 1937. There were 22 members of the lodge who were required to be re-initiated, passed and raised, 20 of whom were re-initiated on the 3rd of November, 1913, with John Mort Snr. – the last Grand Master – leading the rest of the brethren into the ceremony and answering the questions on their behalf. Another member was initiated at a later date, and a block of 18 of the original number received the 2nd and 3rd degrees during meetings held in December and January, with, as Miller puts it in his memoirs, *'a few of the diehards abstaining'*. John Mort Snr. died in March 1928, and was given a Masonic Funeral on the 26th of March, 1928. He continued to wear his Royal Arch apron in lodge meetings despite rejoining the UGLE. John Mort Jnr. resigned due to ill health in January 1933 and died in 1942. Renumbered as 3677, the lodge continued to meet in Wigan, and is still there today.

---

[238] Liverpool Mercury, 7th of October, 1880, issue 10215, p.6.

[239] Liverpool Mercury, 9th of April, 1874, issue 8181, p.6.

[240] Liverpool Mercury, 31st of October, 1867, issue 6165, p.1.

[241] See 'The Transactions of the Odontological Society of Great Britain', Vol.XI, (London: The Society, 1879), p.139. Also see *The Commercial Directory and Shippers Guide 1872*, (Liverpool: R.E. Fulton, 1872), p.174.

Wigan,

BROTHER

I am requested by the Masonic Committee for conducting the Installation of the Grand Officers, &c., on the day of Coronation, to solicit your attendance on that day, and hope you will make application as directed, which will greatly oblige,

Yours,

Fraternally,

ROBERT BOLTON.

CORONATION

OF

QUEEN VICTORIA.

THE GRAND LODGE OF ANCIENT FREE AND ACCEPTED MASONS OF ENGLAND, according to the Old Constitutions granted by His Royal Highness Prince Edwin, at York, Anno Domini 926,—

WILLIAM FARRIMOND, ESQ., Grand Master,—

ON THURSDAY, JUNE 28TH,

(BEING THE DAY APPOINTED FOR THE CORONATION,) THE BRETHREN INTEND TO INSTALL THE GRAND OFFICERS,

ACCORDING TO ANCIENT CUSTOM,

AT THE COMMERCIAL HALL, WIGAN;

From thence to go in Masonic Order (as Master Masons only) to JOIN THE PROCESSION OF THE TOWN, formed in Honour of our ILLUSTRIOUS QUEEN; afterwards to DINE in the said Commercial Hall.

Those Brethren who are desirous of joining the Craft on that day, in their noble design of distributing the blessings of Free Masonry to the Poor and Industrious, as well as to the Noble and Great—whose fundamental principles are to unite the Rich and the Poor in one indissoluble bond of peace and good will towards all men—are requested to make application for Tickets at their LODGE ROOM, Hole-i'th'-Wall, on Monday Evening, June 4th, and on Wednesday Evening, June 13th; to Mr. THOMAS JOHNSON, Hole-i'th'-Wall, or to the SECRETARY, on or before the 22nd of June (if by letter, post-paid.)

ROBERT BOLTON, Grand Secretary.

Wigan, May 23rd, 1838.

J. GRIFFITH, PRINTER, WIGAN.

The advert placed in the Wigan Gazette for the Grand Lodge procession.

The case of the 1839 hand-written version of the 'Magna Charta of Masonic Freedom' specially made for the Grand Master William Farrimond Esq. (Photo by Fred Lomax).

The first page of the rough draft of the Warrant for the Lodge of Truth in Blackburn, 1846.

The gravestone of Charles Wainwright, situated in St. Elphin's churchyard, Warrington, dated 1851. Wainwright was not registered with the UGLE, and the lavish use of the sun and the moon, the all-seeing eye and the set square and compasses are similar to the symbolism used at the time by the Wigan Grand Lodge, suggesting Wainwright may have been a member of the mysterious Lodge of Knowledge.

Leader's Buildings, King Street in Wigan, showing the prominent Masonic symbolism. This was the final meeting place for the Lodge of Sincerity while they were operating under the Grand Lodge of Wigan. (Photo by Fred Lomax).

The lodge room of Sincerity painted by James Miller.

The Royal Arch apron of John Mort Snr., which he wore at all times in the lodge room.

John Mort's name can be seen hand written in ink underneath the top apron flap.

The collar of John Mort Snr.

'Secrets of a Freemason...' – the book used by John Mort Snr. (Photo by Fred Lomax).

James Miller aged 40 in 1921 when he was Worshipful Master of the Lodge of Sincerity. Miller became the last surviving Mason from Sincerity when it was under the Grand Lodge of Wigan, giving his memoirs to Norman Rogers in the late 1940s. (Photo supplied by Miller's Grandson Jim Miller).

Conclusion

The rebellion represented feelings of dissatisfaction and discrimination amongst some Freemasons, especially within the then overlarge Lancashire province. Feeling that their grievances were being unanswered, the rebels made a stand for what they believed was right, and broke away from the United Grand Lodge in London in a desperate attempt to reform the 'Antient' Grand Lodge. The rebellion can also be seen as revolt by a collective of tradesmen from Liverpool and Wigan against the '*tyranny*' of the Duke of Sussex; Freemasons and tradesmen such as Gage, Goepel and Broadhurst seeing the leadership of the United Grand Lodge firmly being in the hands of a London based aristocracy, a leadership that had neglected the issues raised by brethren in the industrial north-west of England, an area which was undoubtedly the largest province in England. This is evident, not only in the actual name of, and the lexicon of language displayed within the '*Magna Charta of Masonic Freedom*' and indeed the 'memorial' to Sussex himself, but also in the aggressive attitude of the leading rebels, some of whom, such as Gage, clearly had personal aspirations, being driven by a heavy concoction of anger and ambition. However, even though it appears that Gage had a lust for power, he also had a vast amount of support, and many Freemasons who were equally as passionate about upholding the rights of their society freely followed him in the revolt.

Many talented Freemasons who served in the rebel Grand Lodge during its existence, such as Gage – who despite having clear personal aspirations and an outright aggressive attitude, was however, an organised and somewhat charismatic leader, and John Mort, whose leadership qualities helped to keep the Wigan Grand Lodge – and indeed the Lodge of Sincerity, alive and functioning during the final years, would never have had an opportunity to serve at Grand Lodge level for the UGLE during this time, mainly because of their locality and their social status. The Grand Masters, and indeed, many of the Grand Officers of the UGLE during this period, were extracted from the Royal family, the aristocracy or were wealthy land owners; normal working men from Wigan and Liverpool would have had a rather slim chance of being elected to an active position. Many Freemasons from Wigan, Liverpool and Warrington could thus demonstrate their leadership and administrative abilities at a Grand Lodge level, albeit a much smaller one than the UGLE in London.

Gage's idea was to recreate the 'Antients'; however, the lacklustre approach to the rebellion by other old 'Antient' lodges throughout England signalled that the rebellion was isolated to the industrial heartland of the northwest. A full blown rebellion was never going to happen after this, and lodges that had initially given support from Yorkshire and other areas of the country such as Kings Lynn, distanced themselves. Even the Barnsley lodge opted out after a number of years. Gage himself became lacklustre, leaving active Freemasonry around 1827, and with a change of career, his attention was placed elsewhere, Gage finally resigning in 1842, effectively rebelling against the rebels.

The rebellion was the last stand of the 'Antients'; the Wigan Grand Lodge actually surviving longer than both the 'Antient' and York Grand Lodges. However, despite the rebellion taking place, the expansion of Freemasonry under the United Grand Lodge of England continued apace during the latter half of the nineteenth century. Though without the rebellion, certain changes would never have taken place; changes such as the dissection of the Lancashire province into the much more manageable Eastern and Western Divisions, the improved communications between lodges, Provincial Grand Lodge and the United Grand Lodge, the enabling of self regulated proceedings within lodges, and other changes in the Book of Constitutions. The spirit of the rebellion lay in the fundamental right of freedom and liberty, and Freemasonry – as a society whose illustrious members have inspired so many throughout the modern era, must always strive to practice that right, lest the spirit of the Liverpool and Wigan rebels may one day rise again.

Appendix I

Magna Charta of Masonic Freedom and Explanatory Information

This is a transcript of the Magna Charta of Masonic Freedom which was originally written in 1823 by the Members of the Grand Lodge of England According to the Old Constitutions, which became known as the Wigan Grand Lodge, and was read annually at the Installation of the Grand Master. This is a re-written version, hand-written by the Grand Secretary Robert Bolton in 1839.

THE MAGNA CHARTA OF MASONIC FREEDOM
FOR THE USE OF THE R.W.G.M.

Presented to W. Farrimond Esq. G.M by the Grand Lodge 1839
Origin and cause of the Re-establishment of the Grand Lodge of Free and Accepted Masons of England according to the Old Constitutions granted by His Royal Highness Prince Edwin at York Anno Domini Nine Hundred Twenty and Six as recorded in the Magna Charta of Masonic Freedom
Copy
In Deo nostrum fidum ponemus
Whereas the two great and Independent Fraternities formerly known under the denomination of Ancient and modern Masons of England did associate themselves by a Treaty of Union bearing date 1st Day of December, 1813 from which period this Grand Incorporated Body was to be known and acknowledged by the Style and Title of the United Grand Lodge of Free and Accepted Masons of England

Therefore be it known unto all whom it may concern that that part of the said United Grand Lodge which is usually held in London have gradually Innovated upon the Ancient Landmarks of Masonry in contravention of the Articles of the aforesaid Union; and they have also composed and published a New code of Laws which are calculated to establish a dangerous and despotic Authority in the Government of our Institution

And furthermore be it known that they have therein introduced a Law for the purpose of enforcing obedience to what is styled by them the established mode of working this new System has been opposed and rejected by an imperative Masonic Duty, because it is not according to the genuine Landmarks Laws and Traditions of the Craft as guaranteed by the third Article of the aforesaid Union but on the contrary it is a compound of Ancient and Modern Masonry filled with <u>new matter</u> and ceremonies to accommodate and reconcile the jarring interests and contentions of those Members who composed the Lodge of Reconciliation thus introducing a system more objectionable than that which divided the Fraternity during the greater part of the last and the present centuries

And be it also known that in consequence of the Innovations which have been thus introduced into the Government of the said United Grand Lodge the fundamental principles & practices of Masonry have been violated; singular outrages and abuses have been committed in different Lodges under the pretence of compelling obedience to the Arbitrary and Illegal commands of a Provincial Grand Master, these proceedings have given use to great animosities, and have created feelings of hostility which are in diametric opposition to the mild and benign spirit of our excellent Institution

Under these circumstances numerous Petitions were sent from various parts of the Kingdom praying for an investigation into the subject matter of complaint; which were so alarming to every Mason who had the welfare of the Craft at heart; instead however of an inquiry being instituted; these petitions were treated with utmost contempt by the aforesaid part of the United Grand Lodge usually held in London, thus affording a strong presumptive proof of their determination to countenance and maintain a Despotic Authority over all Lodges and Masons in this Kingdom

This extraordinary and insufferable conduct caused the Secession of several Lodges and many individual Brethren upon the incontrovertible ground, that the Articles of Masonic Union having been violated, the Contract was thereby broken and the Covenant was thereby dissolved, hence it follows that the United Grand Lodge of Ancient Free and Accepted Masons of England has inevitably ceased to by inevitable consequence ceased to exist

In consideration of this event a general meeting was held at Liverpool on the 21st Day of July 1823 with the Approbation and consent of Lodges No 31, 74, 140, 486 and 521 on the Registry of the late United Grand Lodge, at this Meeting Brother Michael Alexander Gage PM. of Lodge No 31 was unanimously called to the Chair he being the Oldest Master Mason there present who had been Master of a Lodge i.e. according to priority of date

The Chairman having opened the business of the meeting, a full explanation was given of several Innovations and Abuses which had taken place in the Government and Ancient Landmarks of Masonry; the particulars of which (for reasons well known to Ancient Masons) cannot be committed to writing, the Address sent to His Royal Highness the Duke of Sussex in the year 1818 as connected with these subjects, was then fully elucidated, as were also the subsequent communications since made to the Craft at large by which it was satisfactorily proved that not only the Letters but the Spirit-Intent, and meaning of the Aforesaid Articles of Masonic Union had been grossly violated and set at naught

In consequence whereof, the following Resolution were passed unanimously

1   That the genuine Landmarks Laws and Traditions of the Craft have been subverted by that part of the United Grand Lodge of Ancient Free and Accepted Masons of England which is usually held in London in contravention of the Articles of Masonic Union dated the 1st Day of Dec'r 1813

2   That in consequence of the Breach of the Masonic Contract various Lodges and Individual Masons have already Seceded from the Union whereby the United Grand Lodge of Ancient Free and Accepted Masons of England has by inevitable consequence ceased to exist

3   That speedy and effectual measures be adopted in order to re-establish the Grand Lodge of Free and Accepted Masons of England according to the Old Constitutions granted by His Royal Highness Prince Edwin at York Anno Domini Nine Hundred Twenty and Six

4   That in furtherance of the foregoing Resolution the Lodges this day assembled do revert to the Ancient Numbers as expressed in their respective Warrants previous to the Union

5   That this meeting do proceed to Nominate a Grand Master according to Ancient Custom and that his Installation be appointed to take place on or near St. Johns Day the 27th Dec next

Whereupon Brother George Woodcock Esq PM of Lodge No 557 was duly Nominated to fill the duties of that high Office

In conformity with these Resolutions the Grand Lodge assembled in Ample form at Liverpool on the 22nd day of December 1823 when the aforementioned Brother George Woodcock Esq was regularly Proclaimed and Installed according to Ancient Custom Right Worshipful Grand Master of Free and Accepted Masons of England, according to the Old Constitutions after which he received the homage of the Fraternity

The Grand Master having been thus duly nominated, Elected, Proclaimed, and Installed he appointed Worshipful Brother Michael Alexander Gage to be his Deputy; the Grand Assembly then Elected the following Brethren to be Officers of the Grand Lodge for the years ensuing, viz, Brother Ralph Ball Senior Grand

Warden Brother Page Junior Grand Warden Brother Peter Bainbridge Grand Treasurer Brother John Eden Grand Secretary Brother Thomas Roberts Senior Grand Deacon Brother John Thompson Junior Grand Deacon Brother William Green Grand Persuviant and Brother James Ledgeforth Grand Tyler

The Ancient Grand Lodge of Free and Accepted Masons of England being thus firmly re-established, its first effort was directed towards the preservation of the Genuine Laws, Landmarks and Traditions of the Craft in Order that they might be handed down pure and unchanged to the latest posterity

The great and desirable object could only be accomplished by an unequivocal determination to Act and abide by certain defined fundamental Laws of the Institution which cannot hereafter be submitted to Revision or Alteration, under any pretence whatsoever

Therefore we whose names are hereunto subscribed have "solemnly pledged ourselves to <u>Maintain</u>, <u>Uphold</u> and Practise in all time to come the Ancient Landmarks, Usages and Customs of Masonry and Masonic Government; as laid down in the Ancient Constitutions of the Order,"

The manifold disturbances and divisions which have transpired among Masons in every Age and Country; and all feuds Controversies and Animosities which have followed in consequence thereof, may be traced to a departure from the Ancient mode of Masonic Government; the Love of Absolute Power, and the Pride of distinction are among the prominent causes which have led to these unfortunate changes; to obviate which and as a Memento to guard us against the like errors, we have deemed it indispensably necessary to embody in this Instrument, All the Ancient Landmarks of Masonry which respects the government of our Venerable Institution and by which we and our Successors must abide for ever

In testimony whereof we have hereunto Subscribed our Names and Seals this 22nd Day of December in the Year of Our Lord 1823, and in the Year of Light 5827

Ancient Landmarks concerning the Government of Masonry

1   The Ancient and Honourable Fraternity of Free and Accepted Masons have from time to time Immemorial been governed upon a principle peculiar to themselves in which the perfect Representative power is Universally acknowledged

2   The Interests of the Fraternity are managed by a general Representation of all Lodges on Record with the present and past Grand Officers and the Grand Master at their Head; this collective Body is Styled the Grand Lodge

3   The Grand Lodge cannot make any Law or Regulation final and Binding without the express consent of the Majority of Lodges on the record of its Registry; This is the fundamental principle of Masonic Government in order therefore to ensure its strict observance we hereby ordain that every Law or Regulation which may hereafter be made for the General Government of the Fraternity shall be first proposed in writing in open Grand Lodge; and if duly seconded, it shall be faithfully recorded in the minutes thereof, a copy of every such proposition shall be forwarded by the Grand Secretary to every Lodge on the Registry of this Grand Lodge; and it shall be duty of each Master to take an early opportunity of laying such communications before the Lodge over which he may preside; when the sense of his Lodge relative thereto shall have been faithfully taken, it may be conveyed to the next meeting of the Grand Lodge by the proper Representative; or it may be forwarded in Writing to the Grand Secretary being first duly signed by the Master, Wardens, and Secretary, and the Lodge Seal affixed thereto; thus will the true Sense of the whole Fraternity be ascertained in the most impartial manner and the majority of Lodges who may convey their sentiments thereon will render the decision final and Binding and furthermore in order to give the most perfect Satisfaction we also ordain that such decisions with the manner in which each Lodge has voted shall from time to time be regularly communicated to the Craft; as therefore this most important Regulation marks the Power of the Grand Lodge so those written Landmarks do confine within Salutary bounds the power of the whole Fraternity

4   The majority of Lodges cannot destroy the inherent Privileges of the Craft without annihilating themselves as a Body consequently they cannot Delegate the Government of the Fraternity to any Board Committee or Individual however dignified or Respectable

5   The Grand Master must be Elected to rule over the Fraternity according to the Ancient Customs and old established usages of Masonry; consequently neither the Lodges nor their Representatives are authorised to give him Despotic Power nor empower him to appoint others to use it

6   The whole Fraternity are bound in Masonic Allegiance to the Grand Master and the Grand Lodge while they continue to enforce and Act according to these Ancient Landmarks Customs and Usages,

7   The unanimous determination of the Grand Lodge cannot alter the Ancient Landmarks of Masonry

8   The Grand Lodge cannot compel obedience to any System of working in Masonry which was unknown to or not practised by the Ancient Masons of this Kingdom previous to the Union of 1813

9   The Grand Lodge cannot demand general contributions from the Fraternity for any other purpose than to defray the necessary expenses of its establishment

10   The whole Fraternity cannot do that which is forbidden to be done by the Grand Lodge because this Assembly when truly formed according to the 3rd Landmark is a perfect Representation of this Society according to its original Laws, and established Custom

11   Every Master when placed in the Chair shall solemnly Pledge himself to observe all the Old Established Usages and Customs, and to preserve the Ancient Landmarks of the Order, and strictly to enforce them within his own Lodge

12   Every Lodge when duly congregated has an inherent right to regulate its own proceedings provided they are not inconsistent with those points which it is the duty of every Master to enforce according to the proceeding Landmark

13   The majority of every particular Lodge when duly congregated have the privilege of giving instructions to their Master and Wardens previous to the meeting of the Grand Lodge because such Officers are their Representatives and are supposed to speak their Sentiments

14   No petition complaint or remonstrance shall be withheld from the Grand Lodge, upon the ground of its containing indecorous language nor under any other pretence whatsoever

15   No Brother can be either censured or suspended or Expelled from his Lodge until he is convicted after full and impartial investigation of his Offence and it is the duty of every Master to take heed that the Old Hebrew Regulation be strictly adhered to in all subjects of Masonic complaints (Viz) that if a Brother prefer a charge against another and cannot support his charge to Conviction he shall forfeit the same penalty which the accused might have forfeited had he been really convicted, this Ancient Regulation contains the fundamental principle of Masonic Justice and is consecrated by the Sanction of Divine Authority

16 This Magna Charta of Masonic Freedom shall be intrusted to the care and keeping of the Grand Master for the time being, who shall at his Installation renew the solemn engagement herein contained and promise to deliver this Instrument to his Successor after legal nomination Election and Installation according to Ancient Custom

17 That a true copy of this document shall be inserted in the Minute Book of every Lodge upon the Registry of this Grand Lodge

"My Son forget not my Law but let thine heart keep my commandments and remove not the Ancient Landmark which thy Fathers have set."

Solomon

Signed

George Woodcock 557	G.M
M.A Gage 31 & 20	D.G.M
Ralph Ball 492	S.GW
Thomas Page 31	J.G.W
John Eden 20	G.S

P.G Bennett   PM 492
Peter Bainbridge WM 128
John Thompson PM   128
Thomas Roberts SW 20
Robert Hilton Secty 54
Robert Bolton PM 492
Thomas Bullock WM 54
James Cooper PM 54
John Rutter 54
Lawrence Marsden Secty 492
I Sommerville (Scotland) 212
John Molyneaux JW 54
Richard Sayer 492
Wlm Green 54
Thos Strong (Ireland) 548
Wm Marshall 20
Richard Kerfoot 54
Richard Clark 54
Thomas Berry Secty 20
John Page
James Ledgeforth 54

The foregoing is true copy of Magna Charta and examined by me

James Bolton WM
Lodge of Sincerity No 1
Robt Bolton
Grand Secretary

The following is the list of the Grand Officers Elected and Installed June 28th
1838
Willm Farrimond Esq
R.W. Grand Master

Br M A Gage	D.GM
Br Thos Page	S.G.W
Br Jm Golding	J.G.W
Br Ge Daniels	S.G.D
Br Shaw Ellison	J.G.D
Br Jas Walls	G.P
Br Thos Holmes	G.T
Br Robt Bolton	G.S
Br Jas Green	G.T

Appendix II

This is a rough draft for the Warrant for the Lodge of Truth in Blackburn, dated 1846, found within the pages of the main Wigan Grand Lodge minute book. It is an extremely rare example of a Wigan Grand Lodge Warrant, and is hand-written on 3 pages of folded letter paper which is in good condition.

Page 1

To all whom it may concern
We of the Grand Lodge of the most Ancient and Honorable Fraternity of Free and Accepted Masons according to the Old Constitutions granted by his Royal Highness Prince Edwin of York Anno Domini Nine Hundred Twenty and Six and in the year of Masonry Four thousand nine hundred twenty and Six in Ample Form Assembled Viz
The Right Worshipful William Farrimond Esquire of Pemberton near Wigan in the County Palatine of Lancaster Grand Master of Masons
The Right Worshipful John ~~Siddal~~ Glover Deputy Grand Master The Right Worshipful John Siddal Senior Grand Warden The Right Worshipful William Williams Junior Grand Warden with the Approbation and consent of the Warranted Lodges held in this Kingdom according to the Old Constitutions aforesaid do hereby authorise and empower our Trusty and well beloved Brethren viz The Worshipful John Green one of our Master Masons.
The Worshipful John Barber his Senior Warden and The Worshipful Henrey Forrest his Junior Warden to form and hold a Lodge of Free and Accepted Masons aforesaid under the Name and Title of the Lodge of Truth held at the House of Thomas and Alice Stanley

Page 2

Kings Arms Northgate Blackburn in the County Palatine of Lancaster (or elsewhere in Blackburn aforesaid) on every Fourth Saturday and on all Seasonable times and lawful Occasions and in the said Lodge (when duly congregated) to admit and make Free Masons according to the most Ancient and Honorable Custom of the Royal Craft in all Ages and Nations throughout the known World
And We do hereby further authorise and empower our said Trusty and well beloved Brethren John Green John Barber and Henrey Forrest with the consent of the Members of their Lodge to Nominate chuse and install their successors
~~XeXeXeXe Such shall in like manner~~

to whom they shall deliver this Warrant and invest them with their Powers and Dignities as <u>Free Masons Xc</u> and such Successors shall in like manner nominate chuse and install their Successors XcXcXcXc

Such Installation to be upon (or Near) Saint Johns Day during the continuance of this Lodge for ever <u>Provided</u> the above named Brethren and their Successors shall strictly conform to the fundamental Laws and Landmarks of the Order as set forth for the Government of this <u>Grand Lodge</u> in the <u>Magna Charta of Masonic Freedom</u> otherwise this <u>Warrant</u> to be of no force or Virtue

Given under our hands and the Seal of our Grand Lodge in Wigan

Page 3

In the County Palatine of Lancaster this fourteenth day of September in the year of our Lord One thousand Eight hundred forty and Six and in the year of Masonry Five thousand Eight hundred forty and Six

Appendix III

This is a transcription of a letter by John Goulding who was based at the time in Pendleton, north Manchester, to the Grand Secretary Robert Bolton, who was in Wigan. The letter is hand-written on two and a half sides of folded letter paper, dated the 31st of July 1841, and was found within the pages of the main Wigan Grand Lodge minute book. The letter concerns a '*design*' being engraved on copper plate of the Wigan Grand Lodge Certificate, by Mr. Barker of Richmond Street, Manchester. The concept of the Certificate Plate had been proposed at a Grand Lodge meeting on the 4th of June, 1838, and none other than the Deputy Grand Master Michael Alexander Gage had been requested to draw up the design – his artistic talents being called upon.

The letter refers to a Latin inscription using the word '*Constat*' which is a legal term that appears on the actual Wigan Grand Lodge Certificate as transcribed and photographed by Beesley. An example of a Wigan Grand Lodge Certificate can be seen at the Library and Museum of the UGLE. The letter also interestingly refers to the prosperity of No. 1 – the Lodge of Sincerity, and mentions Goulding wishing he could sing the 'Ringley rant' – Ringley being situated near Pendleton, a rant being a lively song sung in Scotland and the north of England. Pilkington, which is also to the north of Manchester, was the location of the Lodge of Faith, which initially supported the rebellion.

Brother John Goulding (written in the minutes as Golding) had served as Junior Grand Warden in 1838, and at the same Grand Lodge meeting mentioned above he had also proposed that Gage be requested to '*frame a Book of Constitutions...and to submit the same in parts to the Grand Lodge for their Approval and be compensated for the same.*' Goulding was again mentioned in a Grand Lodge meeting on the 23rd of December, 1839, proposing that '*a few of the Grand Lodge Officers do meet the Masters and Wardens of the Lodges under this Grand Lodge to form a Code of Laws out of the Ancient Book of Constitutions and the united Grand Lodge Book of Constitutions for the Government of the Ancient Grand Lodge*'. This proposal was seconded by the Grand Secretary Robert Bolton. The spelling and grammar remain the same as the original letter, which is in good condition.

Page 1

Manchester July 31/41

Robert

I have not time to day much at Present but I have this moment called on Mr Barker and with the design which you will recieve when you recieve this note when you look over the Latin part you will find the word Consat which is wrong spelt the word is Constat which Mr Barker corrected I do

Page 2

asure you that he is very attentive and very wishfull to give satisfaction to the Brethren Please to give my sincere regards to the W.M. and the Brethren when you meet on Monday I should have been glad to have been with you but I cannot as I am obliged to be at Pendleton every night and in Manchester in the day it rejoices me to hear of the Prosperity of No. 1 but I would rejoice much more if I could be with you on Monday night

Page 3

to sing Ringley rant for Br Hesketh as I know he likes it
  Hoping you are all well
  I remain yours Pertly
   John Goulding

Bibliography

There are very few publications regarding the Liverpool Masonic Rebellion and the Wigan Grand Lodge. An early mention of the rebellion can be found in R.F. Gould's History of Freemasonry in the 1880s, though the first constructive account came from Eustace Beesley in 1920; a subscription publication which was limited to 500 copies. It was however extremely valuable as Beesley transcribed the main Wigan Grand Lodge minute book and correspondence. Beesley also presented photographs of the 'Magna Charta of Masonic Freedom' taken from the first pages of the main minute book and other documents and artefacts. There were slight mistakes in Beesley's transcriptions, but on the whole his efforts were correct and credible. I have thus chosen to use Beesley's transcriptions in referencing this book as I have seen, studied and compared the original minute book, which is now held in Pemberton Masonic Hall in Wigan, Lancashire. Copies of Beesley's work can still be found in various Masonic libraries around the UK, most notably in the library of the UGLE. C. Gough's work on the Wigan Grand Lodge can also be found in volumes of the MAMR from the early 1920s.

Beesley's work was followed by numerous mentions of the rebellion and the Wigan Grand Lodge in various lodge histories and in four essential academic papers published in AQC; two excellent papers by Norman Rogers – one in 1950 which looked at the 'waste minute book' that Beesley had not seen, and another paper in 1951 which focussed on the lost minutes of the Lodge of Sincerity and the memoirs of James Miller. Some of the events that occurred in Rogers' transcription of the 'waste minute book' can be cross referenced with events displayed in the Lodge of Sincerity minutes. Much later, another interesting paper by Michael Spurr, which was published in 1972, presented an outline of events with selected transcriptions of the earliest Liverpool rebel Committee minute book which Beesley had again not seen. I have also examined the original rebel Committee minute book and Spurr did an excellent presentation of the historical events that took place. This paper was followed in 1978 by Will Read's examination of George Woodcock and the Barnsley based Friendly Lodge; Read examining the minute book and correspondence of the lodge. Read's paper, along with Roger's work, also appeared in volumes of the MAMR.

The memory of the rebellion has been kept alive locally by various Masonic re-enactment teams, entertaining and educating many lodges in the West Lancashire province about the events leading up to the founding of the Wigan Grand Lodge, and by local Masonic historians such as Fred Lomax and Alec Gerrard who have done numerous talks and papers which have included many aspects of the rebellion.

My own previous work on the rebellion includes a number of articles published in MQ magazine and Freemasonry Today, and Chapter 6 of The Transformation of Freemasonry, which details the themes displayed in the rebellion story. A revised and edited version of this chapter appeared as a paper in the THSLC, Vol. 160, after giving a talk on the subject to their society in March 2010.

Primary Source Material

Many of the documents that Beesley had witnessed were sent to the Library and Museum of the UGLE, and on enquiring there in 2000 when I first started my research; I was informed that the professionally written Magna Charta had been lost, even though James Miller had mentioned that he had seen it on the wall of the Grand Librarians private room around the time Norman Rogers had presented his paper on the Lodge of Sincerity to Quatuor Coronati Lodge in 1949. After enquiring again in 2011, I was informed it was in their safe possession, though not catalogued. There were also other items included which are listed here:

Source Material currently held at the UGLE

GBR 1991 HC 4/B "Documents relating to the Liverpool Rebellion, Province of Lancashire, 1801 to 1823." This is a collection of 37 documents containing correspondence, memorials, copy minutes and other documents relating to the early stages of the Liverpool rebellion. Each item has been individually catalogued:

1. Memorial from the Provincial Grand Lodge of Lancashire to the Grand Master
    Creator: Lynch, Daniel
    Call Number: GBR 1991 HC 4/B/1

2. Letter of Daniel Lynch to the Grand Secretaries
    Creator: Lynch, Daniel
    Call Number: GBR 1991 HC 4/B/10

3. Letter of Daniel Lynch to the Grand Secretaries
    Creator: Lynch, Daniel
    Call Number: GBR 1991 HC 4/B/11

4. Copy warrant issued by the Grand Master to William Meyrick, Grand Registrar
    Creator: White, William Henry, 1777-1866
    Call Number: GBR 1991 HC 4/B/12

5.   Letter of Alexander Forrest to Robert Leslie
     Creator: Forrest, Alexander
     Call Number: GBR 1991 HC 4/B/12a

6.   Copy letter of William Meyrick to the Provincial Grand Lodge of Lancashire
     Creator: Meyrick, William
     Call Number: GBR 1991 HC 4/B/13

7.   Letter of William Henry White and Edward Harper to the suspended brethren
     Creator: White, William Henry, 1777-1866
     Creator: Harper, Edwards
     Call Number: GBR 1991 HC 4/B/14

8.   Copy letter of William Meyrick to James Spence
     Creator: Meyrick, William
     Call Number: GBR 1991 HC 4/B/16

9.   Letter of Thomas Berry and others to the Grand Master
     Creator: Berry, Thomas
     Call Number: GBR 1991 HC 4/B/17

10.   Letter of Thomas Mould to the Grand Master
     Creator: Mould, Thomas
     Call Number: GBR 1991 HC 4/B/18

11.   Draft statement of facts concerning the Liverpool rebellion
     Creator: White, William Henry, 1777-1866
     Creator: Harper, Edwards
     Call Number: GBR 1991 HC 4/B/19

12.   List of charges against Thomas Page, sent by Henry Lucas to the Board of General Purposes
     Creator: Lucas, Henry
     Call Number: GBR 1991 HC 4/B/2

13.   Draft paragraph written by the Grand Secretary concerning the Liverpool rebellion
     Creator: White, William Henry, 1777-1866
     Call Number: GBR 1991 HC 4/B/20

14. Draft paragraph written by the Grand Secretary concerning the Liverpool rebellion
    Creator: White, William Henry, 1777-1866
    Call Number: GBR 1991 HC 4/B/21

15. Copy letter of William Henry White to the Lodge of Fidelity, No. 230
    Creator: White, William Henry, 1777-1866
    Call Number: GBR 1991 HC 4/B/22

16. Letter of George Birch to William Meyrick
    Creator: Birch, George
    Call Number: GBR 1991 HC 4/B/23

17. Letter of John Thacker to the Grand Master
    Creator: Thacker, John
    Call Number: GBR 1991 HC 4/B/24

18. Copy minutes of the Ancient Royal Arch Lodge, No. 31 [erased], Liverpool
    Creator: Ancient Royal Arch Lodge, No. 31 [erased], Liverpool
    Call Number: GBR 1991 HC 4/B/25

19. List of brethren present at a meeting of the Ancient Royal Arch Lodge, No. 31 [erased], Liverpool
    Creator: Ancient Royal Arch Lodge, No. 31 [erased], Liverpool
    Call Number: GBR 1991 HC 4/B/26

20. Memorial of the Master and Wardens of the Ancient Royal Arch Lodge, No. 31 [erased], Liverpool
    Creator: Ancient Royal Arch Lodge, No. 31 [erased], Liverpool
    Call Number: GBR 1991 HC 4/B/27

21. Memorial of Thomas Berry and others to Grand Lodge
    Creator: Berry, Thomas
    Call Number: GBR 1991 HC 4/B/28

22. Memorial of Thomas Page and others to the Grand Master
    Creator: Page, Thomas
    Call Number: GBR 1991 HC 4/B/29

23. List of charges against Thomas page, sent by Henry Lucas to Grand Chapter
    Creator: Lucas, Henry
    Call Number: GBR 1991 HC 4/B/3

24. Memorial of Thomas Page and others to Grand Lodge
Creator: Page, Thomas
Call Number: GBR 1991 HC 4/B/30

25. Copy correspondence and documents concerning the Lodges in Liverpool
Creator: Grand Lodge of England
Call Number: GBR 1991 HC 4/B/31 & 32

26. Notice addressed to all the lodges in the province of Lancashire from the Ancient Royal Arch Lodge, No. 31 [erased], Liverpool
Creator: Ancient Royal Arch Lodge, No. 31 [erased], Liverpool
Call Number: GBR 1991 HC 4/B/33

27. Circular letter from the Ancient Royal Arch Lodge, No. 31 and other brethren in Liverpool
Creator: Ancient Royal Arch Lodge, No. 31 [erased], Liverpool
Call Number: GBR 1991 HC 4/B/34

28. Appeal addressed to all the Lodges constituting the Grand Lodge of England from Michael A. Gage and other suspended brethren of Liverpool
Creator: Gage, Michael Alex
Call Number: GBR 1991 HC 4/B/35

29. Refutation of the statements contained in a circular signed by the Grand Secretaries, written by Michael A. Gage and the other suspended brethren in Liverpool
Creator: Gage, Michael Alex
Call Number: GBR 1991 HC 4/B/36

30. Programme of events to be held on one evening at the Star Chamber, Button Street, Liverpool
Creator: Star Chamber, Button Street, Liverpool
Call Number: GBR 1991 HC 4/B/37

31. Circular advertising future publications
Call Number: GBR 1991 HC 4/B/38

32. List of charges against M. A. Gage sent by Henry Lucas to the Board of General Purposes
Creator: Lucas, Henry
Call Number: GBR 1991 HC 4/B/4

33. List of charges against M. A. Gage sent by Henry Lucas to Grand
    Chapter
    Creator: Lucas, Henry
    Call Number: GBR 1991 HC 4/B/5

34. Copy By-laws and other documents relating to the Chapter of the
    Ancient Royal Arch Lodge No. 31[erased], Liverpool
    Creator: Lucas, Henry
    Creator: Ancient Royal Arch Lodge, No. 31 [erased], Liverpool
    Call Number: GBR 1991 HC 4/B/6

35. Letter of William Henry White to Lodge No. 31, Liverpool
    Creator: White, William Henry, 1777-1866
    Call Number: GBR 1991 HC 4/B/7

36. Letter of Peter Parkinson to James Spence
    Creator: Parkinson, Peter
    Call Number: GBR 1991 HC 4/B/8

37. Copy letter of William Henry White, Grand Secretary to Daniel Lynch
    Creator: White, William Henry, 1777-1866
    Call Number: GBR 1991 HC 4/B/9

The are several letters referenced GBR 1991 HC 7/F/6-9 relating to the split in
the Friendly Lodge No. 521, Barnsley, including J.S. Beckett's reply to PGM
Viscount Pollington concerning the return of the lodge warrant, which Beckett
refused to do.

There are two letters from Woodcock to Edwards Harper in the Friendly Lodge
No. 521 file (SN: 1678) both before the split in the lodge (1818 and 1821). One
concerns the laying of a foundation stone of the local church.

There is the un-catalogued copy of the "Magna Charta" of the Grand Lodge of
Wigan. This is a huge document setting down what the rebels think freemasonry
is and is signed by all the leading players in the rebellion including Woodcock as
Grand Master and Gage as Deputy.

There are a couple of certificates for the Wigan Grand Lodge from the late 19th
early 20th century when it was just the Lodge of Sincerity. These are in the
document collection and include the James Miller certificate.

There is also some correspondence from those members of Friendly Lodge, No.
521 who remained loyal to the UGLE after the split. This is kept in the returns

and correspondence covering the years 1814-1830 in the archive store and is held under the lodge number 521.

Other source material relating to the Liverpool Masonic rebellion and the Wigan Grand Lodge:

The first Rebel Committee minute book is held in the archives of Liverpool Masonic Hall, Hope Street, Liverpool, and is not catalogued. This was partly transcribed by Spurr in his paper for AQC in 1972, and is in a good condition. The archives also possess a transcript for the minute book compiled on a typewriter. There is also a file which is not listed, and contains various letters and notes; some refer to the rebellion indirectly – for example, one early lodge summons (included as a photo in this book) has a note to 'Brother Gage' regarding his Grand H.R.A certificate.

The first Grand Lodge minute book is held at Pemberton Masonic Hall, Wigan, and is not catalogued. This was the minute book transcribed by Beesley for his limited edition book published in 1920. It is currently in a good condition, and within its pages it includes four loose letters; there is the rough draft of the Warrant for the Lodge of Truth in Blackburn which is transcribed in appendix II; there is a letter which features two committee meetings – the first on Sunday evening, 6 o'clock, on the 22nd of November, 1840, and the other for the following Sunday evening on the 29th of November, 1840 held at 6.30; there is a letter to Robert Bolton from Brother John Golding dated the 31st of July, 1841 transcribed in appendix III; and the final letter contains the rough minutes for the Grand Lodge meeting on Monday, the 22nd of January, 1844, as seen in Beesley, when the Worshipful Master of Integrity proposed that if any brother makes a proposition to go under the UGLE, they would be fined. They are all in good condition.

The waste minute book of the Wigan Grand Lodge which was partly transcribed by Rogers in his paper for AQC in 1950 is currently missing. It was held by the Lodge of Sincerity, but according to the current Secretary of Sincerity, a number of books went missing after Rogers had studied them, including the original Sincerity minute book. Photostat copies of the lists of membership for the Lodge of Sincerity from the 29th of January, 1787 – 5th of August, 1821, are in the possession of Fred Lomax, and as a note indicates on their cover, they were obtained from *an unsigned source in Wales*. The copies reveal a membership list in a much decayed state that corresponds with Rogers' list in his paper on Sincerity in 1951.

The Magna Charta of Masonic Freedom, 1839, is held at Pemberton Masonic Hall, Wigan, and is not catalogued. It is in good condition and comes in the form of a notebook inserted in a case inscribed to the Grand Master William Farrimond Esq. It has been fully transcribed in Appendix I. The case can be seen in a photo in this book.

Church records for St. Peter's, Church Street, Liverpool 1815-1826. Liverpool Library. Ref: 283PET.

Church records for St. Nicholas, Liverpool, 1817-1842. Liverpool Library. Ref: 283NIC3/12.

Family papers of James Broadhurst. Private collection. Not listed.

Family papers of John Eltonhead. Private collection. Not listed.

List of Members of the Ancient Union Lodge no. 203, 1795-1835, Garston Masonic Hall, Liverpool. Not listed.

List of Members of the Lodge of Lights No.148, Warrington, 1765-1981, Warrington Masonic Hall. Not listed.

List of the Members of Lodge No. 428 (Merchants Lodge), 1789. Liverpool Masonic Hall, Hope Street, Liverpool. Not listed.

List of Members & Minutes of the Lodge of Friendship, No.277, Oldham Masonic Hall, 1789-1900. Not listed.

Minutes of the Lodge of Lights No.148, 1850-1900, Warrington Masonic Hall. Not listed.

Reminiscences of an Unrecognized Lodge, namely Old Sincerity Lodge No. 486 by James Miller, (1959). Many thanks to the Rev. Neville Cryer who supplied the memoirs of James Miller. Not listed.

Dermott, Laurence, *Ahiman Rezon: or A help to all that are, or would be, Free and Accepted Masons,* Second Edition, (London: Robert Black, 1764).

Melville, Herman, *Redburn,* (Harmondsworth: Penguin, 1987).

Lodge Histories
Anon., *A History of the Lodge of Harmony No.220,* (Liverpool, 1948).

Anon. *A Brief History of the Lodge of Perseverance No.155,* (Produced by the lodge and undated).

A History of the "Everton Lodge," No. 823, Liverpool, 1860-1910, (Liverpool: Published by permission of the W. Deputy Provincial Grand Master and by Authority of the Lodge, 1911). 135 pp. This History was the work of a committee consisting of Bros. T. J. Carelull, J. J. Boyle, R. W. Gow, L. G. Davey, W. Griffiths, and other Past Masters of the lodge.

Brown, J., *Masonry in Wigan being a brief history of the Lodge of Antiquity No. 178, Wigan, originally No. 235*, (Wigan: R. Platt, Standishgate and Millgate, 1882).

Hanson, T.W., *The Lodge of Probity No. 61 1738-1938*, (Halifax: Lodge of Probity, 1939).

Macnab, John, *History of the Merchants Lodge No. 241 1780-2004*, Revised and extended edition, (Liverpool, 2004).

Malpus, C.M., *A History of the Royal Lodge of Faith and Friendship, No. 270*, (Berkeley, 2002).

Secondary Material
Anon., 'The Manchester and Liverpool Rail-Road' in the *Monthly Supplement of The Penny Magazine of The Society for the Diffusion of Useful Knowledge*, March 31 to April 30, 1833.

Barker-Cryer, Neville, *York Mysteries Revealed*, (Hersham: Barker-Cryer, 2006).

Bennett, Robert J., *The Voice of Liverpool Business: The First Chamber of Commerce and the Atlantic Economy 1774-c.1796*, (Liverpool: Liverpool Chamber of Commerce, 2010).

Fulford, Roger, *Royal Dukes*, (London: Fontana, 1973).

Gould, Robert Freke, *The History of Freemasonry*, Vol.I-III, (London: Thomas C. Jack, 1883).

Harrison, David, *The Genesis of Freemasonry*, (Hersham: Lewis Masonic, 2009).

Harrison, David, *The Transformation of Freemasonry*, (Bury St. Edmunds: Arima, 2010).

Mackenzie, Kenneth, *The Royal Masonic Cyclopaedia*, (Wellingborough: The Antiquarian Press, 1987).

Sandbach, R.S.E., *Priest and Freemason: The Life of George Oliver*, (Northamptonshire: The Aquarian Press, 1988).

Singer, Arnold, *The Grand Lodge of Wigan 1823-1913*, (Wigan, undated pamphlet).

Journals
Beesley, E.B., 'Undisclosed Records of Another English Grand Lodge' in *MAMR*, Vol. X, (1919-1920).

Gough, C., 'Wigan Grand Lodge', in *MAMR*, Vol. X, (1919-1920).

Gough, C., 'Wigan Grand Lodge', in *MAMR*, Vol. XII, (1921-1922).

Harrison, David, 'Freemasonry, Industry and Charity: The Local Community and the Working Man'. *JIVR*, Volume 5, Number 1, (Winter 2002), pp.33-45.

Harrison, David and Belton, John, 'Society in Flux' in *Researching British Freemasonry 1717-2017: JCRFF*, Vol. 3, (Sheffield : University of Sheffield , 2010), pp.71-99.

Harrison, David, 'The Liverpool Masonic rebellion and the Grand Lodge of Wigan', in *THSLC*, Vol. 160, (2012), pp.67-88.

Read, Will, 'The Spurious Lodge and Chapter at Barnsley ', in *AQC*, Vol. 90, (1978), pp.1-36.

Read, W., 'The Spurious Lodge and RA Chapter at Barnsley', in *MAMR*, Vol. LXVIII, (1978).

Reece, Richard J., 'Thomas Harper', in *AQC*, Vol. 84, (1971), pp.177-186.

Rogers, Norman, 'The Grand Lodge of Wigan', in *MAMR*, Vol. XXXVIII, (1948).

Rogers, Norman, 'Lodge of Sincerity No. 1 (Wigan Grand Lodge)', in *MAMR*, Vol. XXXIX, (1949).

Rogers, Norman, 'The Grand Lodge in Wigan', in *AQC*, Vol. LXI, (1950), pp.170-210.

Rogers, Norman, 'The Lodge of Sincerity, No. 1 of The Wigan Grand Lodge', in *AQC*, Vol. LXII, (1951), pp.33-76.

Sandbach, R.S.E., 'Robert Thomas Crucefix, 1788-1850', in *AQC*, Vol. 102, (1990), pp.134-163.

Spurr, Michael J., 'The Liverpool Rebellion', in *AQC*, Vol. 85, (1972), pp.29-60.

Index

Ancient Union Lodge, Liverpool, 20, 23, 34, 37, 38, 41, 42, 46, 47, 50, 108

Astley, Francis Dukinfield, Provincial Grand Master of Lancashire, 28, 29,40, 42, 43, 76

Beesley, Eustace, B., 27, 38, 58, 70, 99, 101, 102, 107, 109

Berry, Thomas, 23, 41, 42, 47, 50, 51, 95, 103, 104

Bolton, Robert, Grand Secretary of 'Wigan' 1838-1847, 24, 27, 53-56, 59, 61, 67, 89, 95, 96, 99, 107

Bottomley, Masonic ritual, 24, 84, 86

Broadhurst, James, 15, 17, 23, 32-35, 37, 42, 49-51, 87, 108

Castle Inn, North Liverpool, 35, 36, 41, 42

Downshire Lodge, Liverpool, 84

Eden, John, 24, 49-51, 92, 95

Eltonhead, John, 22, 34-36, 42, 47, 54, 108

Everton Lodge, Liverpool, 83, 84, 108

Farrimond, William, second Grand Master of 'Wigan' 1838-1847, 55, 59, 66, 68, 89, 96, 97, 108

Fitzhardinge Berkeley, William 'Bad Billy', 29

Friendly Lodge, Barnsley, 26, 33, 43, 48, 101, 106

Gage, Michael Alexander, Deputy Grand Master of 'Wigan' 1823-1842, 15, 23, 26, 27, 31-33, 35-42, 46-51, 53-55, 57-61, 74-83, 85, 87, 88, 90, 91, 95, 96, 99, 105-107

Gage, Michael Alexander Jnr., 83

George IV, Grand Master of the 'Modern's' 1790-1813, 29

Goepel, John Robert, Snr., 22, 32, 34, 36, 42, 47, 54, 60, 66, 67, 83, 84, 87

Goepel, John Robert, Jnr., 83-86

Goulding, John, 99, 100

Grand Lodge of Stockport, 57, 58

Greetham, James, 39-41

Harbord, Councillor Henry Gordon, 80, 82

Harmonic Lodge, 24, 38, 83

Harper, Thomas, 42, 43, 110

Hawkesley, Thomas, 79

Kent, Duke of, Grand Master of the 'Antient's' in 1813, 42

Knights Templar, 69, 85

Lindsay, Lord, 72, 73

Liverpool Waterworks Bill, 78, 80, 81

Lodge No. 31, (Lodge No. 2), 23, 25, 26, 32, 37, 39-43, 45-48, 55, 58, 66, 75, 104-106

Lodge of Antiquity, London, 18, 42

Lodge of Antiquity, Wigan, 25, 26, 31, 57, 71, 72, 109

Lodge of Friendship, Oldham, 28-30, 48, 108

Lodge of Harmony, Liverpool, 24, 30, 47, 108

Lodge of Harmony and Perseverance, (Lodge No. 3), 58

Lodge of Integrity, (Lodge No. 4), 25, 42, 46, 47, 58, 65

Lodge of Knowledge, (Lodge No. 5), 58, 63-65

Lodge of Lights, Warrington, 28, 64, 65, 108

Lodge of perseverance, Liverpool, 37, 83, 84, 108

Lodge of Sincerity, (Lodge No. 1), 13, 17, 19, 22, 24, 25, 28, 42, 47, 50, 53-55, 57-59, 61, 63-74, 86, 87, 96, 99, 101, 102, 106-108, 110

Lodge of Truth, Blackburn, 58, 97, 107

Lynch, Daniel, Deputy Provincial Grand Master of Lancashire, 28, 39, 41-43, 75, 102, 106

Lucas, Henry, 39-41, 75, 103-106

Magna Charta of Masonic Freedom, 13, 15, 27, 31, 45, 48, 49, 53, 59, 63, 87, 89, 95, 98, 101, 102, 106, 108

Mariners Lodge, Liverpool, 15, 22-24, 36, 37, 41, 42, 47, 48, 84

Mark Masonry, 69

Masonic Manifesto, 24, 31, 35, 36, 42, 53

Merchants Lodge, Liverpool, 13, 15, 23, 24, 30, 34, 35, 37, 41, 42, 50, 54, 84, 108, 109

Meyrick, William, 76, 102-104

Miller, James, 13, 63, 69-74, 86, 101, 102, 106, 108

Mort, John Snr., sixth and final Grand Master of 'Wigan' 1886-1913, 25, 63, 69, 70, 86, 87

Mort, John, Jnr., 71, 86

Page, Thomas, 23, 36, 39, 40, 43, 47, 54, 55, 60, 66, 67, 92, 95, 96, 103-105

Rivington Pike, 78, 79, 81

Rose Bridge Lodge, (Lodge No. 7), 59

Royal Arch, 13, 18, 38, 48, 58, 69, 86, 104-106

Royal Lodge of Faith and Friendship, 30, 109

Santley, Azariah, 24, 35, 42

Sea Captains Lodge, Liverpool, 15, 22, 25, 30, 35, 37, 41, 42, 45, 55

Seddon, Peter, fifth Grand Master of 'Wigan' 1855-1886, 69, 70

Shakespeare Tavern, 27, 48-50, 74

Sickness and Burial fund, 69, 70

Spence, James, 39, 41, 42, 46, 75, 103, 106

St. George's Lodge, Liverpool, 38, 39, 41, 46, 55, 75

St. Paul's Lodge, (Lodge No. 6), 58, 68

St. Peter's Lodge, Liverpool, 84

Staniforth Beckett, John 26, 48, 57

Sussex, Duke of, Grand Master of the UGLE 1813-1843, 18, 27, 38, 41-43, 46, 60, 75, 87, 90

Toxteth Lodge, Liverpool, 24, 84

Unalterable Determination, 31, 35, 42, 53, 54

Wainwright, Charles, 64

Wigan Grand Lodge, 5, 13, 15-17, 25-27, 31, 50, 53-61, 63-74, 78, 86-89, 97, 99, 101, 106, 107, 109, 110

Williams, William, fourth Grand Master of 'Wigan' 1853-1855, 64, 68, 69, 97

Wood, James, third Grand Master of 'Wigan' 1847-1853, 68, 69

Woodcock, George, first Grand Master of 'Wigan' 1823-1827, 22, 26, 32, 33, 43, 48-51, 55, 57, 76, 91, 95, 101, 106

Yachtsman's Lodge, Liverpool, 84

York Grand Lodge, 17, 27, 28, 31, 88

Lightning Source UK Ltd.
Milton Keynes UK
UKHW02f0635181018
330753UK00005B/558/P